A FUNERAL GUIDE

CHRISTIAN HOPE,
CHRISTIAN PRACTICE

A FUNERAL GUIDE

CHRISTIAN HOPE, CHRISTIAN PRACTICE

Ian Markham & Giles Legood

HENDRICKSON PUBLISHERS

Hendrickson Publishers, Inc.
P. O. Box 3473
Peabody, Massachusetts 01961-3473

ISBN 1-56563-923-5

First published in Great Britain in 2003 by the Society for Promoting
Christian Knowledge, Holy Trinity Church, Marylebone Road, London
NW1 4DU.

Printed in the United States of America

First Printing — *January 2004*

The Scripture quotations contained herein are from the New Revised
Standard Version Bible, copyright © 1989 by the Division of Christian
Education of the National Council of the Churches of Christ in the
U.S.A., and are used by permission. All rights reserved.

This publication contains the opinions and ideas of its authors. It is
intended to provide helpful and informative material on the subject cov-
ered. The authors and publisher are not engaged in rendering professional services in this book. The authors and the publisher disclaim any
responsibility for liability, loss, or risk, personal or otherwise, which is in-
curred as a consequence, directly or indirectly, of the use and application
of the contents of this book.

Library of Congress Cataloging-in-Publication Data

Markham, Ian S.
    Christian hope, Christian practice : a funeral guide / Ian Markham
and Giles Legood.
        p. cm.
    Includes bibliographical references.
    ISBN 1-56563-923-5 (pbk. : alk. paper)
    1. Death—Religious aspects—Christianity. 2. Funeral rites and
ceremonies. I. Legood, Giles. II. Title.
    BT825.M315 2003
    265'.85—dc22
                                                    2003015554

To the communities of
Hartford Seminary, Connecticut
and
The Parish of Holy Cross, Bearsted

CONTENTS

INTRODUCTION

The goal of this book is simple: we want to encourage you to think about the reality of death in such a way that you both take seriously the Christian hope and confront all those practical questions. There are many books on the Christian account of eternal life, and there are others on the practicalities of coping with the loss of loved ones and preparing for one's own death, but we have attempted to bring the two worlds together. We believe that all Christians should combine theology with practical preparation. And we hope that readers of this book will appreciate our attempt to do this. It is worth stating right at the outset that this is A *Funeral Guide* primarily for Christians. Although we do touch on attitudes to death in other faith traditions, we are writing for Christians who want to think about the theology and practicalities of their funeral plans.

> **Think about the reality of death in such a way that you both take seriously the Christian hope and confront all those practical questions.**

Death is the one human experience that we can all anticipate with absolute certainty. It is amazing, therefore, that so many people are nervous about talking of death and will do all they can to avoid mentioning the dreaded 'd' word. The authors of this book believe that it is good and healthy to talk about death and dying in the same way that it is good and healthy to talk about some of the other things in life that unite all of humanity: love and relationships.

We would not, however, want to encourage people to be too concerned with thinking about their deaths and the deaths of others (obsessiveness with any subject or idea is rarely a good thing). Nevertheless, we do believe that thinking through some of the issues and choices that have to be made around the time of death, both by those who are dying and by those who care for them, is a good and useful thing to do. There are many big decisions that need to be made at this time, and it is surely better that such decisions are made after considered reflection, thought, and prayer than made quickly. It is hoped that this book will be useful to those thinking through what, if anything, they would like to be done to remember them after their own deaths, as well those who will need a helpful written guide to make decisions on behalf of another after the other's death. In addition, the book should serve the clergy and others in the caring professions. It may be helpful to hand this book to those in need as an introduction and an aid.

Take what is useful to [you in your] own particular circumstances and lay the rest aside.

The book is intended for both selective and systematic reading and raises points for further thought, consideration, and action. We hope that readers will take what is useful to them in their own particular circumstances and lay the rest aside, as is most appropriate. We do not claim that the book is the final word on the subject of funerals, but we have written out of our experience in handling bereavement, both personally and professionally. In our current jobs and in previous working environments, we have walked alongside many going through sad times as we have taught theology and offered pastoral care. In this project, as in much else in life, truth is what works.

Sadly, many of those who have taught us much and shown us real love are no longer with us. We do count ourselves fortunate, however, to have been blessed by the lives of those we loved whom we see no longer and by the lives of our families and friends who surround us today. Their lives, like ours, have been touched and blessed by countless special people who have died. All of these experiences have helped us in the writing of this book. In addition, our awareness of the precious nature of life is heightened by the gifts of Hugh Legood and Luke Markham. We cherish everything they give to us. Furthermore we are enormously grateful to Lesley Markham, whose professional expertise contributed so significantly to the discussion of financial issues which is the subject of chapter 5; to David Barrett who read the American edition with some care; to Barbara Beliveau and Worth Loomis for making various helpful suggestions; and to Yvonne Bowen-Mack and Gwyn Jervis for some much appreciated everyday help and friendship.

Finally, we should like to dedicate this book to two communities. The first has, in recent times, taken one author to another stage on his Christian journey and offered an example of how that faith can be enriched by contact with believers from other faith communities. The other community has sustained one of the authors since birth, setting him on the way and teaching him an immeasurable amount about human life and the Christian faith. Both have given and will continue to give us much to be thankful for.

✍ Chapter One

COPING WITH DEATH

I t was Benjamin Franklin who stated, "In this world nothing can be certain except death and taxes." Today there is an entire industry devoted to worrying about taxes. Newspapers dedicate many column inches to the issue and thousands are employed in either the collection or the avoidance of taxes. Oddly professions concerned with death are much smaller businesses. Churches, of course, take an interest in death, but funeral homes (with some notable exceptions) are often small family firms, and very little space in newspapers and magazines is given over to the issues surrounding death.

Our attitudes toward death are understandable because few people want to think about their mortality.

Such priorities are probably unhealthy. Our attitudes toward death are understandable because few people want to pay even more of their hard earned income to the government and few want to think about their mortality. But such avoidance is unhealthy. Our lack of thought about death makes us unprepared when it strikes. Coping with the death of others needs thought. Coping with the idea of our own death also needs serious thought. We need to prepare ourselves for these inevitabilities. A prepared life, aware of the certainty that everyone we value will one day cease to be, is a life that appreciates the present moment much more. It can and should generate a healthy disposition to life.

Naturally this is not always the case. It is possible to be morbidly preoccupied with death, to take endless fascination in the end of life. As with all questions, a sense of balance and perspective is needed. In the same way as the enjoyment of travel can be distorted by a preoccupation with the possibility of accidents, so the enjoyment of life can be distorted by an obsessive attention to mortality.

The appropriate attitude then is one of balance. In this book we want to explore the reality of death, yet to do so in a way that makes it a constructive part of our lives. For Christians, facing such a reality is part of our calling. We are called to recognize the reality of death, not as the termination of everything that we value, but as a necessary precursor to the growth that God has made possible through eternal life. We are also called to judge our lives in light of death. It is often the case that people who discover that they have only a limited, and known, time to live (for example, coping with a terminal illness) often then realize how much their lives are cluttered with trivial, incidental preoccupations. The next episode of *The Simpsons*, significant though it may be, is definitely less important than a relationship with your children or your partner. Often when we are consciously forced to recognize the limited nature of human life this insight comes into sharp focus.

In life we cope with death in two major ways. The first is the death of other people. There are readers, for instance, who are picking up this book knowing that someone close to them is about to die or perhaps has just died. This might be the first of several times when they will grapple with the death of another. The second way is coping with our own deaths. It might be said that the good thing about one's own death is that at least we do not have to deal with that tragic sense of loss. However, there comes a time in all our lives when we can start to see changes in our bodies, which makes us think about the end of life. Perhaps we are aware that we are unlikely to experience a certain date in the future. Exactly how close that date is to the present time often depends on our age. Forty-year-olds are unlikely to be around sixty years from now. For those who are, say, seventy, just twenty years will see many changes in mobility, independence, and perhaps health. In the rest of this chapter we shall briefly look at how we 'cope' with these aspects of death.

COPING WITH THE DEATH OF OTHERS

All people are born into a complex network of relationships. At birth, we find ourselves surrounded by parents, perhaps brothers and sisters, and perhaps grandparents, uncles, and aunts. Due to the fact that we are social animals, we spend much of our time developing friendships as we grow up. We learn, from childhood onward, the importance of sharing. We find some people whom we like and others whom we find harder to like. With those we like we laugh, smile, share common interests, and look forward to seeing each other. With others, our relationships develop less easily or positively. At their extreme, the latter relationships can be characterized by hate, anger, and hostility.

It is this network of relationships that can make death so significant.

All these relationships define us. If you ask the question "Who am I?" part of the answer will involve the network of relationships that endlessly shape you. To such a question we reply, "I am the daughter of my parents" or "I am the father of my child." Even when we define ourselves around our work, relationships with others are implicit. For example, a response such as "I am an accountant" implies clients, colleagues, and perhaps a boss. When we think about who we are, we find ourselves thinking about relationships with other people.

It is this network of relationships that can make death so significant. Death means that a person around whom many significant relationships exist is no longer with us. There is a significant gap. A link in our network of relationships has disappeared. The extent of that loss ripples out from those most significant to those less significant. With few exceptions, for every person who dies there is a parent, partner, or child who is devastated. There are friends who find their social lives reconfigured and a quality or type of friendship lost (all friendships have their own distinctive quality). Those who knew the person in a professional capacity will also be losing a colleague. At different levels the departed link might provoke ambiguous feelings. Certain relationships are not positive. There are husbands who batter their wives. There are friends who can be draining and destructive. There are bosses at work who are unreasonable and unkind to their employees. In these cases the death of such a person may well provoke very mixed emotions.

In all cases of coping with the death of others, it is important to stress that there is an overwhelming complexity about the loss of a significant person in your life. Acknowledging the complexity of the loss is a good place to start. The most basic lesson is that naming and expressing your feelings is vitally important. Shock and disbelief are common starting points. Anger and guilt often follow. In all cases, the feelings need to be identified and expressed.

This is not a book about bereavement. You will find in the Useful Addresses section at the end of this book lots of suggestions of sources for help with these feelings. The focus of this book is the contribution that the church can make to coping with death (both that of others and your own) and the practicalities surrounding this. However, it is worth briefly looking at the various stages of bereavement, which many experience in their grief.

Many thinkers and writers on bereavement outline seven stages through which the grieving typically pass. These stages do not necessarily occur chronologically, nor do they necessarily all occur. Each person will react to grief in different ways and will manage according to individual personality and needs. Nevertheless the stages are set out for you to consider. The first stage involves a sense of shock and numbness. This is most intense upon hearing of the death and typically can last from a few minutes to several hours. The second stage involves denial where the bereaved person cannot quite believe that the person has actually died. The third stage is characterized by anger that the deceased person has left the bereaved. A sense of guilt defines the fourth stage. This guilt may include the feeling that there is something the bereaved could have done to prevent the death or, more commonly, a sense that there were certain things that needed to be said or unsaid, done or undone.

The stages of grief do not necessarily occur chronologically, nor do they necessarily all occur.

In the fifth stage, a grieving person often bargains. This stage is typical among those who are religious—the religious person will attempt to bargain with God. Depression occurs in the sixth stage when the bereaved person comes to grips with the long-term loss of a significant relationship. The final stage is one of acceptance. It is important to stress that this stage does not mean one is "back to normal." Things will never be the same again and there is a sense in which you never get over the loss of someone close to you. A significant relationship in your network has gone forever. However, you do reach an accommodation with this changed world. This is acceptance.

Funerals often help the process of grieving. Handled properly, they can encourage progress toward the acceptance stage. How this is best done will be a theme of later chapters.

COPING WITH YOUR OWN DEATH

The other potential reader of this book is the person who is increasingly aware of her or his own mortality and wants to make a few preparations. We have already noted that it is both commendable and appropriate to recognize that one day our time on earth will end. This need not be a morbid thought. It is simply facing facts. However, as we reflect further on this fact, we need to recognize that facing such a thought is complicated.

It is, of course, possible that we might die at any moment. Spend an evening listening to the national news and one becomes aware of the tens or hundreds of people who started the morning that day believing that they had a future, only to have their lives tragically terminated. Traffic accidents, natural disasters, murders, and many other things can unnaturally terminate human life. It is right for us to recognize this possibility, but it is also important that we think about this possibility in the light of what is probable. The percentage of people who wake up and who then have their lives ended during the day due to some disaster or misfortune is very small. Television and newspapers mostly report only the important or unusual. Truly representative national news would be very boring indeed. Each day the vast majority of people will get up, do a day's work, come home, and go to bed. The authors of this book know well the cities of Liverpool and London, two relatively dangerous cities. However, most human lives lived in these cities are uneventful—nothing spectacular happens. A healthy recognition of the possibility of a tragic termination of life is right and proper, but it is important to keep it in perspective.

The reason this recognition is healthy is that it encourages us to ensure that everything important to us is correctly ordered. If life ended today, we would be happy with our network of relationships. Sadly sometimes the combination of pride and misunderstanding can damage even very significant relationships. There are parents who are not talking to their children and there are children who are not talking to their siblings (television shows such as Oprah would soon come off the air if this were not so). In the New Testament, Jesus elevates the importance of sorting out relationships before coming to God to repent of one's sins:

So when you are offering your gift at the altar, if you remember that your brother or sister has something against you, leave your gift there before the altar and go; first be reconciled to your brother or sister, and then come and offer your gift. (Matt 5:23–24)

Here Jesus stresses the need for ordered relationships. Making sure that "the sun does not go down on your wrath" is a good principle. This means trying to finish every day with your significant relationships intact and healthy (however infuriating other people might be at times).

Ensuring that in the event of untimely demise our relationships with others are healthy is part of coping with one's own death. However, another aspect is felt by the elderly as they approach the end of life. When humans move into their eighties and nineties, they naturally become much more aware of the precious nature of time and the inevitability of death.

Sadly we live in a culture that does not esteem the elderly. In other parts of the world, the lifetime of wisdom which can be accumulated by the elderly entitles them to respect. The Jewish book of teachings, the Talmud, instructs the young always to stand up in the presence of the elderly. In contrast, Western culture too often celebrates youth to the exclusion of all else. Images on billboards push youth and youthful looks. The elderly are exhorted to make way for the young. It can be very difficult for someone in his fifties to find a job. Ageism, an irrational discrimination against people simply because they are older, is alive and well.

Ensuring that our relationships with others are healthy is part of coping with one's own death.

Recognizing our culture's lack of sympathy toward aging is useful as we consider death and dying. Sending firm signals that as people grow old they are still able to think, make decisions, and enjoy life is important. Elders distinguish between their physical age and the age they feel. Despite the decrease in mobility and the increase in nightly trips to the bathroom, elderly people often talk of feeling as if they were still twenty-one inside. *They* do not think they have changed. Young and old alike should recognize that this is the case. There is often a young person's mind inside an elderly body.

While acknowledging that the appearance of age should not mislead, a shift in relationships must also be recognized. The network of relationships changes as aging moves on. In the passing of time, the chances are that the children have left home, the parent has become a grandparent, the worker has adjusted to retirement, and the anxieties about care when one is very old need to be faced.

It is worth giving significant reflection to these areas because coping with one's own death is largely a matter of ensuring that relationships with those around us are life-enhancing rather than difficult. Changes of roles within a relationship often create major difficulties for those who are elderly. For example, when grandchildren arrive, grandparents' parental roles recede.

Relationships with grandchildren are for most people a complete delight. Grandparents are not required to be the primary disciplinarians of the child, but instead are permitted to gently spoil and indulge the grandchild. While on a day-to-day basis the child's relationship with the parent will go up and down, the grandparent can remain in the background sending out positive and supportive signals. It is not often the relationships with grandchildren themselves that cause problems for grandparents. Rather it is the relationship with the parents, the son or daughter and, of course, the son-in-law and the daughter-in-law. Nevertheless, on the other side of the struggle to let go of the parental role, one of the privileges of old age is that an elderly person can enjoy more freedom than at any other time of his or her life.

THE SHOCKING DEATH

Before we finish this chapter a brief word needs to be addressed to the person who is suffering the loss of a young child or a premature and sudden loss of partner or other loved one. All death is shocking (even the most expected), but some can be especially devastating. In some cases the shock of the death can be almost overwhelming.

A premature death always seems so unjust. Parents expect their children to outlive them. Husbands and wives most often marry expecting to share old age with each other. To have these lives and expectations suddenly cut short is very difficult. More often than not, there is no short cut to being able to "get over" such deaths. The grief and pain, which will be considerable, must simply be lived through. Space to weep, rage, and pray is essential. In the short term, the goal will be to cope. Awareness of the extent of the pain is key to dealing with an unexpected death (as it is with other death, too). One should never underestimate the extent of healing required.

Yet a "good funeral" (and yes, the phrase is deliberately odd) can be an important part of the healing process. You will need to try to take control of as much as you can. Involve yourself in the details of planning the funeral. Make sure the send-off is appropriate to you, but also recognize that you will be one person among many who are hurting deeply.

Embarking on This Book

Thus far we have tried to meet readers wherever they are. You might be reading this book, sensitive to the friend or relative who has died, and therefore in need of help to arrange the funeral. You might be reading this book because you are aware of the nearing inevitability of a death, either your own or that of another person. Whatever position you find yourself in, part of the secret of a happy life is to accept the universal reality that human life is finite. Whatever position you find yourself in, there is hope.

Prayer for Those Who Have Recently Lost a Loved One

God our Creator, who brought us to birth and in whose arms we die, comfort all who mourn the loss of (name). Embrace us with your tender love, give us hope for new life in the days and weeks ahead, and help us see that with you nothing is wasted or incomplete. This we ask in the name of him who died for us, Jesus Christ, your Son, our Lord. Amen.

Prayer for Those Who Are Aware of Growing Old

Eternal God, who through the ages remains the same, be near to me as I grow old. Though my body fails, let my mind be strong and my faith in you endure, so that with patience I may bear all things, believe all things, hope all things, endure all things, and at the last may meet death unafraid, through Jesus Christ our Lord. Amen.

Prayer for Those in a State of Shock

O God, you rule over your creation with tenderness, offering fresh hope in the midst of the most terrible misery. We pray for all those whose souls are blackened by despair. Infuse them with the pure light of your love, shower on them your gentleness that even in their darkest moments they may be open to your love and bring kindness to one another and to themselves. Amen.

✍ Chapter Two

FUNERALS AND DEATH

In chapter 1 we looked at the themes of aging and death. In this chapter we shall start to explore the relationship of death and dying to the funeral. There is a long and complicated history to this relationship, so we begin with a brief history of various rites that surround death. After this we shall go global and look at the different ways in which the transition from life to death has been marked. The next part of this chapter will consider those ways of dying that may create particularly sensitive issues for the funeral. Finally, the chapter present the specifically Christian dimension of funerals and see how and where the Christian rites are located.

THE HISTORY OF DEATH RITES

Douglas Davies in his masterful study *Death, Ritual, and Belief*[1] explains that probably the first form of funeral was the act of burying a person in the floor of a cave. Indeed there is archaeological evidence of this going right back to the early Stone Age (some thirty thousand years ago). The idea of marking the point of burial also has a significant history. In Malta, for example, there are two-thousand-year-old stone structures that probably represent a memorial to the deceased. There is also considerable evidence that earlier funeral rites had a dual role, first to disentangle the life of the person who had died from this world and second to establish the person in the life to come. This remains a feature of the Greek Orthodox ritual. Here the first stage is the burial of the body, where it is left for several years to decay. The second stage is the removal of the skeleton to an ossuary, a special building for the holding of bones.

Each type of funeral has a different set of symbols and expectations.

While burial is probably the oldest form of funeral, the practice of burning the body (or cremation) also has a venerable history. It almost certainly can be traced to Ancient Greece (evidence for the practice has been found from two thousand years ago). In addition, there are well-documented examples of cremation being the practice for warriors who died in war. Cremation facilitated returning the remains of a dead soldier back to the town or village from which he came.

Along with stone-marked burial and cremation, there were other forms of dealing with a dead body. Perhaps the most famous example of an alternative is the Lindow Man, probably a highly respected Briton who died during the period of the Druids eighteen hundred years ago. He was placed in a peat bog, which, as it happened, preserved his body so effectively that one can see precisely how he died.

The fact that marking the disposal of mortal remains has such a long history should not surprise us. It is undoubtedly a very significant moment. Each type of funeral has a different set of symbols and expectations (some of which we shall look at later in this book). Most aspects of the modern funeral have roots in antiquity. However, one exception is the modern practice of the funeral home, in which the undertaker transforms and prepares the body. Up until the middle of the nineteenth century, the family handled the arrangements concerning the body after death. An undertaker was one who undertook to handle the arrangements. The participation of undertakers, increasingly known as funeral directors, is now a feature of the modern funeral, and the service provided can be extremely helpful to those who are coping with a death.

THE GROWING POPULARITY OF CREMATION

Later in this book we will look at the arguments for and against cremation and burial. At this point it is important simply to document the growing popularity of cremation and some of the reasons for this.

In the United States, approximately twenty-five percent of funerals are cremations. The Cremation Association of North America estimates that by 2010, forty-seven percent of funerals will be cremations. Although increasingly popular, this estimate is probably optimistic. It is true, however, that in European countries, such as the U.K., cremation is now the most popular form of funeral.

Even for funeral services in the church, it is common in the U.K. for a brief service of committal to follow the crematorium. Unlike other European countries, in the U.K. the actual burning of the body takes place out of sight of the mourners. Following cremation the next of kin must decide what they want to happen to the ashes. Some simply leave it to the crematorium to place them in the "Garden of Remembrance." Others may ask for the ashes to be returned. They are then free to distribute them however they wish. Disposal of ashes may include placing them under a tree in the garden, having them scattered over the sea or perhaps taken to a favorite place of the person who died.

There are a number of reasons for the growth in popularity of cremation. First, it is seen as more eco-friendly. Burial of a body requires more space than that of ashes. Second, many mourners are attracted by the possibility of having the ashes to do with what they will. It creates some attractive possibilities and perhaps may mean that the remains of the person who has just died can be blended into the environment in a host of different settings (for example, in a meadow, a wood, or the ocean). Third, for some it is felt that it helps with the healing process for those who are grieving as there will not necessarily be a grave, which some might feel obliged to visit.

On the other hand, the debates over cremation have been the subject of some controversy, even causing diplomatic incidents.[2] In the 1950s the Chinese, appalled at the Russian treatment of the hero of the Russian Revolution, Lenin, insisted that in the future all senior Chinese officials must be cremated. Lenin had been embalmed and his body was placed on public display in a special mausoleum in Red Square. The Chinese felt that something akin to a cult had developed around Lenin and his tomb. Communist leaders in Hungary combined the two and cremated the bodies of leaders, preserving the ashes in a vast, purpose-built edifice. The ashes of Mahatma Gandhi caused a political crisis in India when, in 1996, some were found in a bank vault in Orissa. Although some of his ashes had been sent to various sacred rivers in India, the rest had simply been stored away. The problem was finally resolved with the decision of the Indian government to place the remaining ashes in the River Ganges.

GOING GLOBAL

All practices in human life arise from a certain context with a certain significance. One can learn a great deal from the exercise of comparison and contrast. Often it is only in seeing how a different culture handles an issue that one appreciates the symbolism and purpose of one's own culture. For example, a person who has been brought up a Roman Catholic may find a visit to a Quaker meeting with its simplicity and silence a very quick way of appreciating the purpose and symbolism of the visitor's own Roman Catholic liturgy. Travel, either physical or imaginary, does indeed broaden the mind.

Let us now take an imaginary journey starting in China. China is especially interesting because there ancestors are given a major place in the extraordinary mix that makes up Chinese religion. Here one will find three stages. The first is the burial. Given this is the least important of the three stages, the place of burial does not matter a great deal. The purpose of this stage is to wait for the body to decompose. The second stage, then, is to inter the bones in an appropriate container. This container or urn might be reburied to await the third stage, when the container is placed in a permanent tomb.

At the second stage, the person's name is added to the ancestral list. This might be simply a list kept at home, but sometimes it will be a list kept in an ancestor hall. The entire rite is organized around the significance of the ancestor. For this culture, one's sense of belonging is not just immediate (i.e. the mother and father or sister and brother) but is also firmly located in the wider context of the past and the future. Chinese culture has a strong sense of one's immediate family, but this includes all those who have gone before, not just those who are around us here and now. Much of the religious year in China is organized around "respect" to the ancestors. They are a continuing part of the lives of the living.

Now let us take a second journey, this time to the city of Benares on the River Ganges. What will we find there? Douglas Davies provides a summary:

The basic pattern of the death ritual is, at one level, quite simple. Dying persons should be laid on the ground with

> prayers chanted to help them focus on the name of God
> as they die. After death, the body is washed, dressed and
> carried home for cremation. During the cremation the
> skull is cracked by the eldest surviving son . . . after the
> cremation the remains are thrown into the river.[3]

This simple procedure is rich in symbolism. In Hindu mythology a person is a combination of flesh, which comes from the menstrual flow of the mother, and bones, which come from the semen of the father. As a baby grows in the womb, it is believed that the heat of the mother enables that growth. After five months of growth in the womb, the life force enters the baby through its head. Douglas explains how the rituals surrounding death mirror this birth process:

> Death, symbolically speaking, parallels this pattern of
> birth for just as the maternal heat helps produce the
> foetus so the heat of the cremation fire destroys the
> flesh, leaving the bones behind. It is as though the ele-
> ments derived from the female are destroyed, along with
> the sin of the individual, which is symbolically associ-
> ated with body hair, itself also destroyed by fire. The re-
> maining bones are placed in the river which is associated
> with the female principle of existence and thereby, in a
> symbolic sense, becomes a fertilizing agent. . . . Just as
> the spirit comes to the baby in the womb through its
> skull so now it departs, through the skull, as the skull is
> cracked during cremation.[4]

The ritual surrounding death is a mirror of the process of birth. As life has been received in the cycle of birth and rebirth, so this life ends and is passed on to be reborn.

Although we have focused on the rich Hindu symbolism of birth and death, India is probably better known, in ritual terms, for the practice of sati. This occurs when the grieving widow decides to join her husband on the funeral pyre and is thus cremated with him. There is considerable argument among scholars whether this practice really is encouraged in the religious tradition. In the Hindu scriptures, the Rig Veda, there is a rite where the woman is described as lying next to her dead husband but then leaving the pyre to go to his living brother. Elsewhere there is a passage that promises great "glory" for a woman who undergoes this practice.

Numerous rulers and many religious Hindu leaders have opposed the practice of sati. It is a custom now completely illegal in modern India, although there are reports that it still occasionally takes place. It should be stressed that such practice was fairly rare, and today almost everyone thinks of such as suicide and therefore entirely inappropriate.

Before we consider suicide in more detail, it is worth pausing and considering what we can learn from our imaginary journey. From China, we can see the importance of the family tree. In America today there are tens of thousands of people who spend significant portions of their free time locating themselves and their children in the context of their own family trees. There are computer programs and websites specially dedicated to helping these genealogists in their task. Others spend their time visiting cemeteries and looking at church records in an attempt to find out what happened to some distant ancestor. It might be that locating ourselves in such a family context is an aspect that we ought to take into account when thinking about planning the details of funerals.

From India, we can see the importance of considering together birth and death. The rituals of death and dying feed the obvious observation that as babies are born so other human beings at the very same moment are dying. Hinduism can teach us that it is entirely right to see that birth and death in this life go hand in hand. There is a natural rhythm to birth, death, and new life.

SUICIDE AND EUTHANASIA

The Indian practice of sati raised an issue that obviously needs some treatment in a book such as this. Suicide can take many different forms. At its most dramatic, it can involve a suicide bomber who is willing to sacrifice his (or occasionally her) life to end the lives of a perceived enemy or to make a political point. More often, suicide is the deed of an individual person, acting alone, to curtail his or her own life. The reasons for such cases can be many, ranging from a strong sense of anger to a sense of hopelessness and despair.

The Christian tradition has largely felt that suicide is wrong, as it is not the same as self-sacrifice. Self-sacrifice occurs when one's prime motive is not to seek death, but to save others and in doing so one sacrifices one's own life. Captain Lawrence Oates famously left his tent during an Antarctic expedition, explaining as he did so that he was "just going outside and [might] be some time" in order to free up supplies for his fellow travelers. The reason suicide generally is wrong is that life is a precious and privileged gift. It is a blessed privilege to have life. Granted, life does have its dark sides, but the expectation and hope of Christianity is that life will be rich in its range of experiences. The gift of life is not something that anyone chooses or earns, it is simply that, a "gift," granted by the mysterious processes of being. For those who are feeling suicidal, Christian hope can be found in working with others to find healing. Desperate situations can be converted to hopeful ones.

Voluntary euthanasia is a form of legalized suicide. There is only one country in the world—the Netherlands—that has legalized euthanasia. The conditions for granting a request for euthanasia there are very strict. They require that the patient must have a terminal illness, that the patient must have made repeated requests for euthanasia, and the authorities and relatives must have been informed.

Most Christians are opposed to the legalization of euthanasia. In the United States, most doctors do not want to become people who terminate life. Their training and practice is directed toward the saving of lives, not their taking. The majority of doctors feel that the legal power to assist in euthanasia might send potentially mixed messages to patients. Most people, they believe, want to know that their doctors are in the business of making people better, not killing them. In addition, there is some concern that it is difficult to be sure the decision made by the patient is not

> **Life does have its dark sides, but the expectation and hope of Christianity is that life will be rich in its range of experiences.**

coerced. Many elderly people go through phases of feeling that they are useless or a burden and a drain on the resources of their children and family. To live in a culture where an unscrupulous child, eager for the inheritance, could apply pressure to an old person to sign up for euthanasia would be undesirable.

However, the strongest argument against euthanasia is the dramatic progress in palliative care, which stops attempting to cure the patient, but instead concentrates on ameliorating the symptoms. In other words, terminally ill patients get to the point where they are clear that that they will not recover. They will then be offered palliative care, which in the U.S. and U.K. will take place in a hospice, a day center, or at home. Palliative care is primarily pain management. One of the remarkable features of the modern day is that pain can be managed so effectively that the vast majority can expect to have, at least physically, a pain-free death. As life approaches the very end, it is not uncommon for a physician to recommend dosages of medication that will ultimately terminate the life of the patient. However, it is important to note that this is not necessarily hastening death. Pain management, not only calms the patient, but it can extend life, even when the dosages are very high.

For this reason, in the U.S., there is virtual agreement among the medical, nursing, and religious professions concerning the value and importance of palliative care. Although some states have expressed sympathy with a law permitting assisted suicide or voluntary euthanasia, the majority have felt that to introduce a voluntary euthanasia law or to raise the possibility of such acts being sanctioned through the law courts is very undesirable.

CONCLUDING CHRISTIAN REFLECTIONS

As we have seen, the need to mark the occasion of death has a long history and is found in a host of different cultures. The vast majority of cultures do not see death as the end, but rather see it either as a way for the soul to return in a new and different body or as a doorway into a different mode of being.

In the next chapter we will look at the Christian account of this alternate manner of being. However, at the end of this chapter, we need to locate speculations concerning the afterlife in the framework of life. What do Christians claim for this life?

It is wrong to imagine that Christianity is primarily a set of beliefs about the life to come. It is not. It is first and foremost a way of living here and now. The Christian tradition teaches that the great privilege of life, the privilege of breathing and existing moment to moment, is not an accident, but intended. Even if human life evolved from simpler forms, we need not necessarily assume that the whole process is simply a cosmic accident. Instead, Christians may believe that at the heart of the universe is goodness and love. This is primarily what Christians mean by the word "God." The nature of love

involves the desire to create more "loving possibilities," and these possibilities are one of the reasons
people choose to have babies. Here, a couple love
each other so much that they express their love for
each other by creating another person, who in turn
supplements and enhances that love. In the Christian drama God creates new life. God has allowed
sentient and complex creatures such as humankind
to emerge. As humans, our purpose in being is to
discover love and to express love. In this process of
discovering love, we create things that Christians
believe will last forever.

A Christian hope, therefore, of life beyond the
grave should not diminish the importance of life.
Because life matters ultimately, this life here and
now matters immediately. Human life
becomes more significant because we **Because life matters**
are called to account for the love we **ultimately, this life**
discover and generate as well as for, **here and now**
conversely, the selfishness and ha- **matters**
tred we cause. Some people imagine **immediately.**
that belief in life after death is partly
responsible for the damage that human beings
cause in this world. After the World Trade Center
terrorism, Richard Dawkins, a biologist teaching at
Oxford University, complained:

> If death is final, a rational agent can be expected to
> value his life highly and be reluctant to risk it. This
> makes the world a safer place, just as a plane is safer if its
> hijacker wants to survive. At the other extreme, if a sig-
> nificant number of people convince themselves, or are
> convinced by their priests, that a martyr's death is equiv-
> alent to pressing the hyperspace button and zooming
> through a wormhole to another universe, it can make the
> world a very dangerous place.[5]

Dawkins is right to draw attention to the dark potential of religion. The Christian hope must never be used as an incentive to inflict pain and hurt on others. The Christian story (and, incidentally, the Islamic one) insists that the slaughter of the innocent is a blasphemy against God. The life of Jesus himself prioritized love. However, Dawkins is wrong to imagine that atheists are never going to commit suicide or opt for a misguided set of ideals that require self-sacrifice. Plenty of atheists died for an atheist ideology called Communism. The truth is that both atheists and religious people need to recognize the value of this life and the importance of building up loving relationships within it.

The gift of life has been granted, a life has been lived, and a life has now ended. These facts in themselves are enough to demonstrate why the end of a human life should be marked.

The focus of a Christian funeral, therefore, should very much be the celebration of the life lived. From the very young, who often give much more than is appreciated, to those who have lived a long life with significant achievements, there should be a celebration of the gift and triumph of that life. The Christian hope is that in most lives there is material that God can use to build the person in eternity. For Christians, this is what it means to believe in life after death. In the next chapter we shall speculate a little on whether this belief makes sense in the modern world. Whether it does or does not, however, the Christian understandings of both the funeral and the value of this life persist. A funeral marks a substantial moment even if there is nothing beyond. There are plenty of good reasons to commemorate the end of life with ritual even if death is the end of that individual person. The gift of life has been granted, a life has been lived, and a life has now ended. These facts in themselves are enough to demonstrate why the end of a human life should be marked.

✍ Chapter Three
CHRISTIANITY AND DEATH

G iven that death is universal, it is not surprising that there are many different explanations about what exactly happens at death. We all agree that biologically the heart stops beating and mental activity ceases, but beyond that there is considerable disagreement. Indeed historically and geographically, we find a vast array of accounts of death. In India, for instance, reincarnation is the dominant view. This view believes that death is simply a bridge where the soul leaves one person to become reincarnated into another person's body. For Christians and Muslims, however, the traditional view has been that each unique soul will find itself either in heaven or in hell.

In parts of the Western world today, there is a widespread view that death is the end. Some thinkers believe that this is not only scientifically more plausible, but also ethically superior. The advantage of insisting "this is it" is that one will focus all the more effectively on this life. Indeed Karl Marx's great complaint about life after death was that for the poor and oppressed it became a great hope that eased their acceptance of the injustices of this life.

Marx wanted the poor to stop hoping for life beyond the grave and start sorting life out here and now. Religion, he said, was the opiate of the people.

All Christians would concede the wrong of misusing a guarantee of life beyond the grave as an excuse for not changing life here and now. For some Christians, there is a sense that Christianity should be more focused on life here and now and less worried about life after death. Such Christians would point to the way in which the expression "eternal life" is used in John's Gospel. There, eternal life is seen, not as a state in heaven, but as a quality of life that starts now. This Johannine view equates being faithful to God in this life with discovering those supreme values that God represents and living them as fully as possible.

However, for other Christians, life is part of a bigger picture. Participation of this life in a greater whole grants value to this earthly existence. Love matters simply because it matters eternally. People matter ultimately because they are created to partake in the life of God for eternity. Immortality counts because it becomes the context in which we determine what ultimately concerns us.

For most Christians, the main reason they believe in some survival beyond the grave is the resurrection of Jesus. St. Paul claimed that "if Christ has not been raised, then our proclamation has been in vain and your faith has been in vain" (1 Cor 15:14). The Jesus movement developed because those around him believed that he had conquered death.

Furthermore, most Christians are committed to believing that we live on beyond death because it helps explain how and why evil and suffering are permitted. If there was no bigger picture, then most explanations would sound very feeble. "Suffering builds character" works only in a limited way. It becomes obscene when confronting issues such as rape, child abuse, or serial murder. Too often in such situations character is destroyed. In short, those values that are possible only through suffering become cruelly absurd when death takes the sufferer to oblivion. This is not to say that "pie in the sky" somehow justifies suffering, but rather that the ways in which values are discovered through suffering have an eternal significance. Suffering is organically connected to its results in the individual's life and the fruition of those results in eternity.

Most Christians are committed to believing that we live on beyond death because it helps explain how and why evil and suffering are permitted.

The only way these eternal values can be discovered is through suffering. Acknowledging this organic connection provides a perspective for suffering that enables us to see that the values emerging from suffering are precious.

For many people hope that makes sense of human suffering is sufficient and they do not need to wrestle with details about how this works. However, for others it is important to think through how these things can be possible. The next section covers some of these details. If such issues hold little interest for you, however, please feel free to skip the next section and move on to the end of the chapter.

WHAT IT MEANS TO BE HUMAN

For Christians, one fundamental of their faith is that all humans are created in the image of God. This sounds straightforward, but what exactly does it mean? Does it mean that we are different from all the (non-human) animals? For some critics of Christianity, this is a very problematic doctrine. They ask, "Why should humans think they are so special?" Two groups in particular have raised certain difficulties with the idea that humans are made in the image of God.

The first is the "deep ecology" group. Shallow ecology worries about the environment to make sure that humans still have a planet to enjoy. Deep ecology is committed to the planet because the planet itself has intrinsic, independent value. Value, for deep ecologists, is not imposed from outside—from the human perspective. Rather, each part of the environment has its own place and role and is acknowledged to be equally as significant and equally as precious as the rest. From this point of view, only human conceit claims that humans are more significant than hedgehogs or mountains. Furthermore, deep ecologists argue, such conceit is deeply damaging. Under the banner of human preeminence, humans use and destroy animals, plants and geology.

We can and should affirm the concern that underpins deep ecology, but we also want to affirm the doctrine that humans are made in God's image. To insist that everything is equally significant rapidly becomes a nonsense. A carrot is important, but morally it is correctly seen as less important than a dog. Dogs have feelings and capacities for relationships that carrots do not. It is the complexity of a dog that entitles it to more rights and greater care. For all the reasons that dogs exceed carrots, so humans exceed dogs. This is a point we will return to in a moment.

There is a second objection that needs to be discussed. It comes from the Australian philosopher Peter Singer. Singer has coined the expression "speciesism" to describe the vice of valuing one species over others for no good reason. The reasons that people normally cite for preferring humans to other living things are the intelligence, moral awareness, language, and capacity for thought that humans possess. Not all humans, however, have all these attributes. Babies, the severely mentally ill, and the very old may not have the same powers of speech or intelligence as other human beings. Non-human animals (especially the higher primates) have much better communication and powers of reasoning than human babies. We do not, however, exclude babies and include gorillas in our preferences because of this. Such choices, Peter Singer says, expose the affirmation of the human as a prejudice: Christians are guilty of speciesism.

We can and should affirm the concern that underpins deep ecology, but we also want to affirm the doctrine that humans are made in God's image.

Singer is right to insist that some of the important characteristics of the human species are found outside the human community. Dolphins are highly intelligent, for instance; and the higher primates can, in some respects, mirror human communities. This leads us to believe that there is a sliding scale of rights. According to this scale humans are more significant than any other form of life, but gorillas and dolphins are more significant than say mice, while mice are more significant than daisies. Other animals and plants should be judged against these same criteria.

Singer, however, is wrong to define a species by the less developed and mal-developed. To do that would be like defining an eye with respect to blindness, simply because some eyes, tragically, do not operate properly. Babies have a potential that gorillas do not. Those elderly humans who deteriorate so much that speech becomes impossible or those who are born with severe Down's syndrome are, in part, analogous to those who are asleep. Keith Ward, the English theologian, makes the point well when he writes:

> Just as a person who is asleep does not use his or her rational powers, so a mentally handicapped person is prevented from using such powers, often throughout a whole lifetime. The subject of their consciousness is not non-human, or that proper to an animal. It is human, belonging to the human species, but is deprived of its proper form of activity.[1]

Humanity should be defined by the characteristics true of humans in their normal mode; that is, developed, awake, and well. When we are less developed or asleep or ill, we are still human, even if we are unable to use and enjoy all the capacities and gifts of being human.

It is important to defend this concept against, for example, those responsible for concentration camps during the Second World War. That people are made in God's image explains why an indifferent attitude toward human life is evil. But it also supports concern for ecology. We have been created with the capacity to use our power for good or ill. This is what bearing "God's image" means. The privilege of being human involves responsibility. If humans have no greater value, and therefore no greater rights and responsibilities, than any other part of the environment, then to criticize and exhort humans to behave more responsibly becomes a nonsense. For the ecological crisis to be tackled, we need to persuade more people that we have the power to adjust our priorities and to act justly toward the environment.

So far, we have defended the idea of the image of God from objections. But what else ought we to say about it? The doctrine has its roots in the famous opening chapter of the Bible, which reads:

> Then God said, "Let us make humankind in our image, according to our likeness; and let them have dominion over the fish of the sea, and over the birds of the air, and over the cattle, and over all the wild animals of the earth, and over every creeping thing that creeps upon the earth." So God created humankind in his image. (Gen 1:26–27)

In a special way humans share something of the creative power and responsibilities of the Creator. What exactly does this mean? Among the early church fathers (leaders who formulated much of Christian doctrine in the early centuries of the church), there was a difference of emphasis. Augustine stressed human reason, which reflected the wisdom of God, while Athanasius emphasized humankind's unique potential for relationship with God. Both of these strands are important and should be linked. Human reason and our capacity for relationships depend on

- the capacity for language, which is the distinctive gift of reason,
- the capacity for love and intimacy, supremely with God,
- the gift of freedom, and
- our moral awareness.

Language marks out the human species. Clearly other animals have a limited range of signals and noises that provide basic forms of communication, but human language is unique in its effectiveness. Experience is organized, evaluated, and controlled through language. It is a precondition for all other human activities. Relationships that transcend the instinctive—that warrant the language of love—are also a marked feature of human communities. We can give ourselves to others and share each other's lives. This is true, not only on the human level, but also on the divine. Freedom is a prerequisite of love. One cannot love if one is compelled. To use an analogy, it is very easy to set up one's computer with a loving message on the screen saver, but the message lacks profound significance precisely because it has been programmed. One does not value a declaration of love from a machine. The capacity to choose and take responsibility for choice is an important element of being human. Love is the expression of freedom.

Moral capacity is implied in the above, yet it stands alone in embracing all those defining decisions that determine our openness to love or self. Language, our capacity for relationships, freedom, and moral discernment are all the defining characteristics of being human. They are thus the reasons it is a privilege to be human. This then is earthly human life, made in the image of God, but what happens after we die?

LIVING FOR ETERNITY

Of course, no one knows for sure what life beyond the grave is going to be like. We are at this point forced to resort to "revelation" (i.e. some source that religious people believe has authority because it reveals God to us). Different religious traditions have given different accounts of the content of this divine revelation. If one asks a Hindu, for example, she will give a different answer from that of a Christian. Furthermore, different types of Hindu or different types of Christian will give different answers while speaking from the same religious traditions. There is no uniform, universal, Christian position. It is, however, worth noting at this point that the answers given by different religious traditions are not completely different. Most traditions stress some element of judgment (that we must take responsibility for the decisions made in this life). Most also aspire to some state of harmony, where love and freedom finally coincide, where the radical flaws in earthly life are absent. However, even with these broad areas of agreement, there are significant differences. What follows is one picture of what "eternal life" means. It is one that we believe makes sense, but it is also one with which others will disagree.

As Christians we turn to the resources of our tradition. Life after death is relatively unimportant in the Hebrew Bible (the Old Testament). In the texts that make up this part of the Bible, God's judgment of the nations tends to occur in this world alone.

The Gospels take the resurrection of Jesus to be a model of the general resurrection to come. The Christian Scriptures (the New Testament) however, were written when expectations of the end of the world, coupled with a general resurrection, were widespread. Such beliefs became central themes within the New Testament since they were all written in light of the resurrection of Jesus.

The precise nature of the historical event that underpins the story told after Jesus' death is now unobtainable to us. We cannot get behind the differing descriptions of his resurrection in the first letter to the Corinthians and in the Gospels according to Matthew, Mark, Luke, and John. All the authors of these texts agree that the experience is "real" and life transforming. They also take the resurrection of Jesus to be a model of the general resurrection to come. From this, perhaps, we can work out the following.

On the whole, the Christian tradition has been committed to a view of humanity that some philosophers call a "psychosomatic unity." This rather complicated technical terminology simply means that people consist of a body and soul that are integrated and unified. That the body is useless but the soul survives death is not the dominant view of the church. Philosophically, this picture of a disembodied soul is difficult to understand. For most Christians, when they imagine life beyond the grave, they imagine a state in which humans have a mental life (i.e. thoughts, etc.) located within a body. This is what St. Paul saw as a transformed self. The precise nature of the body is difficult to describe. Just as there is a different flesh for animals and humans, so there will be different bodies for life on earth and life in heaven (see 1 Cor 15:39). It seems reasonable that individuals' bodies in heaven will operate differently from their present ones in some significant way. Presumably such a state would require a space-time framework in which we will not be subject to the bodily restrictions that we currently endure.

This brief sketch is grounded in the New Testament talk about resurrection.

This brief sketch is grounded in the New Testament talk about resurrection. Philosophically there is a big problem with life beyond the grave because of the death gap. This death gap makes certain identification very difficult. How do we know that the person who earlier today drank a cup of coffee is the same person who is reading this chapter now? One very good answer is that there has been bodily continuity. In other words, the bundle of atoms that comprise "you" continues to exist in space and time from when you had your earlier cup of coffee to now reading this page. Some philosophers, however, find it difficult to imagine personal identity overcoming these gaps in bodily continuity.

In order to help answer this problem let us imagine a thought exercise (one that is adapted from the contemporary English philosopher Keith Ward). Suppose that all children, at the age of eight, suddenly disappear for two minutes and then reappear as humanoid birds. The process undergone is much like a caterpillar changing into a butterfly, but with a short gap to enable the transformation to take place. Now, while this sounds odd to us, if it were universal it would appear completely normal. The humanoid bird would share many of the characteristics of the child. It would remember being a child. It would have the same basic character and personality as the child. However, once it became a humanoid bird, its character would inevitably change, in much the same way as the character of a person who recovers the ability to walk after being confined to a wheelchair for ten years changes. The point being made by Ward is simple. If this were merely a part of the natural process, we would rapidly become accustomed to talking about the humanoid bird as identical to the child. If the process went wrong, which from time to time it probably would, and two humanoid birds emerged, then we would probably talk about the child splitting into two birds and require that each should be treated as an autonomous individual.

Keith Ward suggests that life beyond the grave will involve a similar change. After death our characters will transfer from our existing bodies into heavenly bodies. These heavenly bodies will enable different capacities that will bring about change and development in our characters.

This picture is loosely built on the resurrection of Jesus. Many Christians think it makes sense to imagine a resurrection, with a mind in a body, operating in a space-time framework, in which individuals will be recognizable. However, thus far in this chapter we have considered eternal life involving only humankind. What about the rest of creation?

A REDEEMED CREATION

For some Christians, the doctrine of the creation of the world seems more attractive than that of the redemption of the world. Creation consists of the whole of the cosmic order (with the earth as one small part of it). It is rich in its diversity and beauty. In contrast, however, redemption at the end of time seems confined to humankind. In questioning such a view the writers of this book cannot help but wonder why God bothered with animals and plants and the rest of creation if the end result involves their exclusion. Surely we should expect the scale of redemption to be at least equivalent to that of creation.

In the letter to the Romans in the New Testament, St. Paul insists that the "creation itself will be set free from its bondage to decay and will obtain the freedom of the glory of the children of God" (Rom

8:21). The book of Revelation talks about a "new heaven and a new earth" (Rev 21:1). In addition to the more narrow view of redemption in the paragraph above, there is a strong strand in the Christian tradition that holds that all of creation will ultimately be redeemed. We think this strand should be taken seriously.

While admitting that all talk concerning the end of time and what happens after death is speculative, it does seem reasonable to believe that in some way, analogous to the normal developing and changing of a human life in the here and now, all matter and life will be transformed at the end of time. One of the great theologians of the twentieth century, Jürgen Moltmann, brought the significance of Jesus' resurrection together with a cosmic view that justified the redemption of the entire creation. He wrote:

If the day of Christ's resurrection is the first day of the new creation, then it also brings the creation of new light, a light which lights up not merely sense but the mind and spirit too, and shines over the whole new creation.

In the Epistle to the Colossians a vision of cosmic peace is developed which is grounded on a cosmic christology. Through Christ everything will be reconciled "whether on earth or in heaven, making peace by the blood of his cross" (1:20).

He [Christ] died . . . so as to reconcile everything in heaven and on earth, which means the angels and the beasts too, and to bring peace to the whole creation.

If Christ has died not merely for the reconciliation of human beings, but for the reconciliation of all other creatures too, then every created being enjoys infinite value in God's sight, and has its own right to live; this is not true of human beings alone.[2]

In short, Moltmann argues, if Jesus died for the whole world, then we should reasonably expect the whole world to be redeemed at the end of time. In some sense, animals, plants and the whole of creation will have a place in the life to come.

HELL

For many as they approach death, it is not the hope of heaven that preoccupies them, but the fear of hell. Hell is the state of unrelenting punishment by God for the wickedness that we have done on earth. For some Christians, hell is believed to be the destination for all those who are not Christians.

Although it is true that we will all have to face up to the consequences of our behavior on earth, we are not persuaded about such a reality as hell. The problems with such a straightforward doctrine of hell seem overwhelming. To divide humanity into those deserving of heaven and those deserving of hell seems impossible. There are plenty of Christians who thwart love while there are equally plenty of nonbelievers who exhibit all the "fruits of the spirit" (love and kindness, etc.) that St. Paul talks about (Gal 5:22). An eternity of punishment seems disproportionate for a lifetime of wickedness, even if one has been exceptionally wicked. Beside this, the Christian good news (the gospel) is about Christ dying for the whole world so that the whole world is redeemed.

In our view, hell as traditionally described is very unlikely. Instead we, like many Christians, see hell as a state of selfishness and loneliness that we create for ourselves. Hell is very much a state of mind that we can and do create here on earth. As we discover love, so we discover the life of God, and as we create barriers of hatred, so we create hell. It is possible that when we die some of us, perhaps most of us, will still have barriers that will need destroying. This is the problematic area that the doctrine of purgatory set out to resolve. It would be wrong to get too mathematical and attempt to calculate precisely the time in purgatory that each sin is likely to accrue. Instead it is our view that human barriers created by individuals need to be destroyed by love, and that this process should start in this life and might require some time in the life to come to bring it to completion.

By the time the funeral comes about, the destination of that person's essence is in the hands of God.

ALL THIS AND THE FUNERAL

These reflections and speculations set the scene in which the funeral takes place, although at the time they may seem peripheral to the process of organizing the funeral. By the time the funeral comes about, the destination of that person's essence is in the hands of God. At such time we simply trust that the Creator of the universe will do right. We do not need to, nor should we, speculate about the likely nature of life beyond the grave.

Yet we have included our analysis (and we stress that it is simply our view—there are plenty of alternative accounts) because we do believe that the funeral should be viewed as a positive occasion. It is, if you like, the doorway to transformation. As we will see later in the book, in addition to being a time for sorrow, the funeral ought to be a celebration of the life lived and an occasion for great hope. The hope will be that all the problems that make up a human life are caught up in the drama of God's redemption and transformed into building blocks for the occasion of love.

The Christian hope is important. We need constantly to retain the sense that our lives are a small part of a greater whole. Only from this perspective can much that appears difficult and odd now ultimately form a pattern that can be used by God for eternity.

✍ Chapter Four
ATTITUDES TOWARD DEATH

Thinking about dying and death can be difficult because our Western culture has removed death from the agenda of much of life. Where once our forebears lived with death around them each week, today most deaths take place in hospitals. Our modern attitude could be characterized as "out of sight out of mind." As talking of sex was once the big taboo, today talking about death is avoided by many. In addition to the reticence of people to see death as natural and unavoidable, many see it as something to be ashamed of or regard death as a failure of medical science. When death *is* talked about in Western society, it is often done in an unhealthy and sometimes damaging way. Modern Western culture seems to have generated a set of beliefs that are untrue and unhelpful in coming to terms with death and dying. Our task in this chapter is to name these false beliefs and explain precisely why they should be challenged and replaced with something better.

Thinking about dying and death can be difficult because our Western culture has removed death from the agenda of much of life.

Although Christians are confident of hope in life that triumphs over death, there is still a sense of loss here and now. This is a loss that we will live with until we ourselves die. We do not need to remove it from our feelings, nor should we be ashamed about it. How we handle that sense of loss will depend on a multitude of factors, individual and rarely easy to manage.

FALSE BELIEF ONE

It is easier to cope with the death of an old person than the death of a young person.
Even though this is understandable, it is nevertheless mistaken. There is a sense of horror when death strikes the very young. The death of a child is a crippling tragedy; the sudden loss of potential and the destruction of innocence leaves a deep sense of bewilderment. What is not the case, however, is that because the death of a young person is tragic, then the death of an older person is less terrible and is therefore easier to deal with. Just because someone dies in his or her eighties or nineties does not necessarily mean that it should be more easily handled.

When someone dies in their eighties or nineties, there is a lifetime of patterns that have grown up around that person. Indeed, the sense that a parent will always be around and part of your life has been generated. For decades (perhaps eight or nine decades) that person has been a significant part of your life, and the connections with her or him have become part of your own identity. It is easy to take for granted that your parent (or other loved one) will be around forever just as the sun, moon, planets, and stars will revolve throughout your whole life. You don't wake up each morning worrying about the continuing planetary positions, and this same attitude is assumed toward your elderly relative or friend.

The death of both young and old can be deeply traumatic.

A young person's death is not trivial, but the death of both young and old can be deeply traumatic. The observation "At least Fred had a rich and fulfilling life" is often unhelpful. This is no compensation for the gap left in the life of those who survived. Acknowledging this gap is an important aspect in the process of accepting the death and moving on with one's own life.

FALSE BELIEF TWO

An unexpected death is harder to cope with than one that results from a long illness.

This misconception plays to an intuition that, in emotional terms, shock is harder than preparation and that a deep traumatic shock involving the sudden death of a loved one can be very difficult. A death resulting from a car accident or sudden heart attack, where the person dies almost instantaneously, provides no opportunity for the final goodbye, a last cuddle or squeeze of the hand. In living busy lives, it is easy to start the working day without demonstrating the underlying love we feel for those close to us. In such circumstances the unexpected death seems so harsh and capricious that it seems bound to be harder to cope with than the one prepared for death.

However, what such an attitude overlooks is that sustained periods of illness also bring their own stresses and demands. Watching the gradual deterioration of a loved one can be a heart-wrenching obligation. Illness can distort the personality. In illnesses parts of a personality, such as a great sense of humor, may disappear behind the person's daily struggles to cope with the pain she feels. Perhaps the lively mind that has engaged the world with great vitality becomes muddled and confused. Living with illness can be extremely difficult both for those who are suffering and for those who are watching and caring.

In addition to the anguish that accompanies waiting comes the feeling of hope. The numerous opportunities for preparedness that this period of illness affords can disappear underneath an unrealistic hope that recovery is imminent. New medical technologies will be tried; prayer and other hopes to bring about recovery will be invoked. All this can lead to the further strain of endless false dawns and with them accompanying frustration.

Finally, a long, sustained illness can leave deep scars of guilt. It is not uncommon for both the person dying and those watching to find the language of euthanasia or even the passing thought of suicide a temptation. One might almost feel "relieved" that death has been the final release from pain. This relief now can become a problem later if guilt—

wondering how authentic the love they felt really was—compounds grief. Again, the truth is that both shocking death and death after a sustained period of illness are difficult to handle. Both bring their distinctive problems, which will need to be confronted and handled with sensitivity.

FALSE BELIEF THREE

People find it easier to handle bereavement when they are older.

It is much harder to cope with death when one is younger. Losing a parent in one's teenage years seems so manifestly tragic that one imagines it must be easier to cope with the death of a parent when one is aged, say, sixty. It is easy to think that the teenager has enjoyed the relationship for only a limited number of years and that, in addition, he lacks the resources maturity brings to locate and place the tragedy into perspective.

Yet what such an attitude ignores is that maturity is a limited aid for coping with these uniquely sad moments in life. Maturity is helpful in handling repeated problems in life. For instance, the romance that fails after a couple of days and seems the "end of the world" for a teen can be dealt with wholly differently by a thirty-year-old because it is only one of many moments of unrequited love. However, the death of a parent is not a "repeat" problem, which can be coped with better each time. Similarly, the death of other relatives or friends is no substitute for the unique way in which each of their particular deaths might touch you. Maturity gives you no preparation for the unique tragedy and gap that a particular death can bring.

FALSE BELIEF FOUR

You are finally "over" the death of a loved one when you start to enjoy life again.

This perhaps is the most pernicious false belief of all. It works in a variety of different ways. It is possible for someone to die and for a grieving person to see the funny side to life twenty-four hours later. This does not mean, however, that the bereaved person is indifferent to the tragedy. Coping with bereavement is a highly individual process, and the true impact is felt perhaps only months or years later. Conversely, it is true that for some people the sense of shock and numbness leaves them deeply preoccupied and unable to laugh at anything in life for the time being.

Maturity gives you no preparation for the unique tragedy and gap that a particular death can bring.

The point here is simple: one should always seek to recognize how one feels and should not deny that or behave in a way that feels unnatural or false. If one is feeling anger, then it is right that this anger is expressed in some way. If one is feeling sad, then a "good cry" might be precisely what is needed. Also if the bereaved person wants to smile, to laugh, or to crack a joke, then she should feel free to do so. It is important not to let the expectations of those around you determine how you behave (although it is right that you are sensitive to other people around you, who may also be bereaved). In the end each individual has to come to grips with loss in his own way and is entitled to find and use whatever reasonable means of coping best helps him.

Later in this book we shall look at the different kinds of funerals that help people mourn a death and express what is felt about the deceased person. One of the purposes of this comparative exercise will be to reinforce the simple point that much of our cultural conditioning (the way Western culture has shaped our thinking) can be problematic. Some find it helpful to consider the experiences of other cultures in dealing with death and dying. Doing so can expose us to the alternatives and make us think about the appropriateness of our own assumptions. When we look at how some Western people have adapted death rituals, as with all material in this book, do not feel obliged to read it. This is a handbook, which can be dipped in and out of. It is not intended as a manual for all people to use in all circumstances. Readers should feel free to skip any section and move on to those they find more helpful or applicable for their particular circumstances.

Some find it helpful to consider the experiences of other cultures in dealing with death and dying.

✍ Chapter Five
FINANCIAL MATTERS

In this chapter, our attention will turn once again to focus on the person preparing for her or his own death. We will deal with the practical questions that surround the legal documents such as the will, and those that are concerned with finances. Before such issues are examined, however, we begin by pausing and giving some thought to the appropriateness or otherwise of Christians worrying about monetary matters.

One immediate problem which might arise for some Christians is found in the Sermon on the Mount, which is a central part of Jesus' teaching (Matt 5–7). Here Jesus taught, "Do not worry about tomorrow, for tomorrow will bring worries of its own. Today's trouble is enough for today" (Matt 6:34). He also said, "Look at the birds of the air; they neither sow nor reap nor gather into barns, and yet your heavenly Father feeds them. Are you not of more value than they?" (Matt 6:26). In these passages Jesus stresses keeping these practical arrangements in perspective. Life, Jesus says, is more than worrying about what we will wear or what we will eat and drink.

Every day on the television news or in the newspapers we find examples of devastated lives, where the "best laid plans of mice and men" do not work. In the end we have to live by trust. We have to trust that the world will remain fundamentally ordered and that it will remain trustworthy. We should not imagine that we will be able to foresee every possible eventuality of action or inaction. There are a million and one things that could happen that we cannot anticipate and cannot protect ourselves or our loved ones from. Every day as we wake, as far as is reasonably possible, it is appropriate to be thankful. We can be grateful to find ourselves in a home, when many do not. We can be grateful that the day is relatively predictable, when for many the day is anything but. And we should be grateful that at the end of the day, it is likely we will climb back into the same bed. There are many people over the centuries and—to the world's shame—today, who have not enjoyed such good fortune and privilege.

> **There are a million and one things that could happen that we cannot anticipate and cannot protect ourselves or our loved ones from. Every day as we wake, as far as is reasonably possible, it is appropriate to be thankful.**

So with the sense that Christians do their planning tentatively (and gratefully), we can now embark on the exercise of planning with which this chapter is concerned. As in all life, big or small, Christians should try to place their financial planning within the context of prayer. In deciding how to use your money (whether that is a large or small amount), you are making some important decisions that may affect significantly the lives of those whom you leave behind.

FACING UP TO THE FINANCIAL IMPLICATIONS

Many people have concerns about the financial impact their deaths will have upon their loved ones. Most also have a good idea of whom they wish to receive any money or assets from the estate, be it family, friends, or charities. However, actually putting legal documentation in place to carry out these wishes can seem like a minefield to many.

There are several aspects to consider:

- obtaining life insurance
- making a will
- choosing executors
- managing estate taxes
- paying for the funeral

We will consider each of these topics in turn. This book is not intended to advise you on these highly technical areas, and we recommend that you seek help from a financial advisor, an attorney, an accountant, or all three. The purpose of this chapter, however, is to highlight the areas that you should consider, either in preparation of your own affairs, or as an executor of a will. It will serve as a good introduction to the subjects and a useful background for you before you see a professional in those fields.[1]

LIFE INSURANCE

Life insurance comes in many shapes and forms and is offered by a large number of companies. It can be complicated deciding which, if any, is best for you, but a financial advisor or life insurance agent should be able to help in this process.

The two main types of life insurance are "term" and "whole life." Term insurance provides a certain amount of coverage for an annual premium; it does not have a cash value and pays out should death occur during the premium period. A whole life policy also pays a death benefit, but it develops a cash value since part of the premiums are invested and part are used for the life cover, so in effect, it includes a savings account.

Insurance proceeds paid on death are not subject to income tax on the beneficiary. Whether you need life insurance will probably depend on your age and the size of your debts, if any. The most likely candidates are those with mortgages and/or children of school age and younger. Life insurance might be used to pay off the mortgage and leave an amount for any dependent spouse, partner, or children to live on. A retired couple that has fully paid their mortgage may be less likely to require substantial life insurance. However, even in this case, a surviving spouse will still need sufficient income to pay funeral expenses and to maintain his or her lifestyle without selling the house for income.

Life insurance is also a useful tool in estate planning. Some people take out life insurance to ensure that their estate remains "liquid," providing cash to pay any taxes and other creditors in order to preserve the estate intact for the beneficiaries. The provision of cash to pay liabilities prevents the need to sell assets within the estate prior to their distribution to the beneficiaries. Life insurance can also be viewed as a method of increasing the value of an inherited estate for the cost of the premiums.

A WILL

Most people discuss with others their wishes for the distribution of their estate. "Estate" means the total amount of money and assets a person leaves upon death. It is, however, vital that these wishes are written down in a legal document. This legal document is a will, and it must be properly executed in the presence of two witnesses (some states require three) who are not beneficiaries. You must be sure that your executors know where the will is kept. Often it is best to retain the will with the attorney who drafted it. Do not leave it in a safe deposit box since some states seal the boxes upon death, which can delay matters considerably. You should also consider updating your will every few years to ensure that it still reflects your wishes. It may be that further children or grandchildren have been born or that beneficiaries have died or that tax laws have changed significantly since you last revised your will.

Some people take out life insurance to ensure that their estate remains liquid.

If you die without a will, you die "intestate." Your estate will then be distributed according to the laws of intestacy, which may not reflect your wishes. The intestacy laws vary among states and usually attempt to provide for your family first, but they will not take into account a friend or favorite charity or your desired division among relatives. While we have noted that states vary, the general pattern is for property to pass half to the spouse and the remaining half among the children. If there is no spouse or child, the property passes to parents and then to grandparents and more remote relatives. Where there are children and the spouse "shares" the estate with them, the laws of intestacy could leave the surviving spouse with too little income since a significant proportion of the estate has passed directly to the children. Drafting a will yourself is possible if your affairs are relatively straightforward.

If there is no spouse or child, the property passes to parents.

There are many books, computer software packages, and websites[2] that show you how to write your own will. However, there could be pitfalls in drawing it up yourself since it needs to be legally correct. If in doubt, seek advice from an expert. It is important to recognize which assets will be governed by the will and are thus considered part of your "probate" estate. Generally the only assets governed by a will are those where the title is individually owned. This can exclude joint assets such as homes owned jointly and joint bank accounts. Any life insurance policies or retirement plans with beneficiaries named in the policy may also be excluded from the probate estate. For these types of reasons, even a simple scenario may need more careful consideration. It may be possible and desirable to leave no probate estate. The alternative is to ask an attorney to draw up a will for you. Ask for a quote before you proceed; the cost should reflect the complexity of your personal circumstances.

It is also important to make a will if you have children under eighteen or who are disabled because you should appoint a guardian (and an alternate guardian if the first cannot act), who would take care of them if you die without a partner or your partner dies with you. With many children living with step-parents, it is not always clear who should be the guardian if a natural parent dies. This is a difficult topic to raise, but it is essential for the children to be considered. A judge will ultimately decide who should become guardian, but the decision will be made in light of your wishes as stated in your will.

EXECUTORS

An executor is the person who will administer your will and ensure that your wishes are carried out. The executor is sometimes referred to as the administrator or personal representative. Typically a judge appoints an administrator in the case of an intestate estate. The executor may liaise with an attorney to ensure that the estate is correctly distributed and that tax obligations have been appropriately satisfied. It is necessary to "admit the will to probate," the state court procedure to administer the deceased's will and to ensure that it has been properly made and carried out. This process must be performed before the estate can be distributed. The executor will then collect and distribute cash and property and pay debts and taxes. Once the estate has been distributed, the court approves the final account and terminates probate.

People commonly choose a relative to be the executor. You will need to select an executor capable of dealing with the complexities of the job. It is advisable to have a backup executor in case the first cannot or will not serve. While a relative is often the person who knows best what the will-writer's ("testator's") intentions were, you should bear in mind the stress that accompanies death. Being executor may be too much for some relatives to manage. You may consider appointing your bank or attorney as executor or possibly as joint executor with a family member. This relieves some of the pressure from relatives and is certainly a major consideration if there are likely to be disputes over the will or if there are technical issues involved. A professional executor is likely to charge a fee.

ESTATE TAXES

The federal gift tax is a tax that is potentially payable on gifts made during your lifetime. The federal estate tax is potentially payable upon death. Estate tax and gift tax need to be viewed together since the final estate tax is generally based upon taxable transfers during life combined with the value of the estate at death. However, anyone may contribute up to eleven thousand dollars per year to each child (or anyone else) without either donor or donee having to file or pay any tax. You should take this into account in your estate planning. Estate and gift tax (and generation-skipping tax described briefly below) are federal taxes; some states also impose an inheritance tax or estate tax on their residents.

Federal estate tax is a hot topic in the government, and the tax may well be reformed or even abolished. We have attempted to set out below the current situation at writing, but it is an area that may well change in the near future, and you should therefore check for any changes in the law.

Federal estate tax is payable once an estate exceeds the lifetime exemption threshold. The threshold is increasing annually to three and a half million dollars by 2009 with no federal estate tax in 2010. In 2011 it will revert back to one million dollars unless new legislation is introduced. Legislation is in flux, and it is advisable to check for changes affecting the later years. The threshold for 2003 is one million dollars. The excess estate is taxed on a graduated scale at rates rising from forty-one percent to forty-nine percent. The lifetime exemption is reduced by any taxable gifts made during your lifetime. If you make gifts of say five hundred thousand dollars during your lifetime, you will have only five hundred thousand dollars left as an exemption at death. The lifetime exemption can be reached more easily than you imagine, especially for people who own their own home. The value of any pension and life insurance may also be included. So, many more people can be caught in the estate tax net than it would originally appear. Current market values of all assets at death must be reported to the IRS so that any estate taxes due can be determined. There are generally no estate taxes payable on assets that pass between husband and wife; this is referred to as the marital deduction. You should consult an expert if either husband or wife was born outside of the U.S. or is not a U.S. citizen since the tax treatment could be significantly different.

Current market values of all assets at death must be reported to the IRS so that any estate taxes due can be determined.

Amounts that have accumulated in nontaxable Keogh retirement plans, IRA, 401K, and other accounts are subject to very high rates of taxation if they remain in the estate of a single person or the last spouse to die. This is because such assets may be subject to both income tax and estate tax. Accordingly, it may be desirable to leave all or some of these assets to a charitable organization, thereby avoiding any tax. (Of course, the value of the estate is reduced by the bequest.) This is another reason to consult an expert.

It is possible for any person to gift up to eleven thousand dollars to one or more persons each year without the gift being included in your lifetime exemption. This is referred to as the annual exclusion. This is a useful tool and enables, for example, each parent to give money and assets up to eleven thousand dollars to each child and grandchild each year without compromising the exemption. There are special reliefs available for qualifying family-owned business interests. It is strongly recommended that professional advice be sought under these circumstances to ensure that the relief is applicable and is used to the full where available. Amounts left to charity are eligible for a deduction from your estate. There are certain tax planning alternatives that attempt to reduce your estate tax liability, many involving trusts. Your accountant, attorney, tax advisor, or financial adviser can be of service if you think these deductions may be applicable to you. You will undoubtedly be charged for the advice, but it could save considerable amounts of tax and keep your bequests more intact. We noted above that there is no tax payable on transfers between husband and wife. However, when the second spouse dies there will be a charge on the whole remaining estate. If the first spouse to die leaves his or her entire estate outright to the survivor, the first spouse does not, in effect, utilize the lifetime exemption. Instead, perhaps, some of the value of the estate (up to the lifetime exemption) can be used on the first death, for example, not leaving all assets to the spouse but leaving some to the children as well, or putting in place a trust that will allow the exemption to be used. Again this is advisable only if it is put into place correctly and allows the surviving spouse to live comfortably. There are trusts that enable the surviving spouse to live off the income of assets although the actual assets no longer belong legally to that person.

There are certain tax planning alternatives that attempt to reduce your estate tax liability, many involving trusts.

On the federal level, there may be an additional generation-skipping tax (assessed at the highest federal estate tax rate and subject to its own additional exemption) upon transfers during lifetime or at death to persons two or more generations below the transferor. Outright gifts to grandchildren in amounts of eleven thousand dollars or less are generally not subject to the generation-skipping tax, but particular caution should be exercised in contemplating substantial gifts to grandchildren or others two or more generations younger than the transferor.

State inheritance or estate tax varies enormously. Rates are generally lower but may also begin to apply at a lower threshold than the one million dollars federal estate tax. They can still produce a sizable tax bill. You will usually be liable for state taxes in the state in which you are a permanent resident. Some states also charge estate tax on real estate and tangible personal property situated within the state boundaries but owned by nonresidents.

State taxes are imposed in a similar way to federal estate taxes and may be subject to some exemptions such as tax-free transfers between husband and wife. It is not our intention to cover all of the individual state taxes, and it is worth looking at your state's department of revenues website to determine the rules which will apply to you. Some states base their estate tax upon the federal death tax credit. So where federal estate tax is payable, the state will charge tax equal to the federal death tax credit. There are tables available which calculate the federal death tax credit according to the size of your estate. Some estates have an inheritance tax that is computed on the recipient of the estate.

FUNERAL EXPENSES

While it is not necessary for a person to think about the payment for his or her own funeral, nevertheless many people do make provision for this so as not to burden their nearest and dearest with extra work or expense. Prepaid funeral contracts, offered by most funeral homes, allow customers to make choices about the type of funeral they want for themselves (something this book encourages), to see that these arrangements will be carried through by a specific funeral home, and to pay for this in advance. They also allow you to shop around for the best deal, comparing prices. This is something that your relatives are unlikely to do after your death, before arranging your funeral.

There are drawbacks to such schemes. The funeral home may not act honorably or the funeral home may be sold and the new owner not honor your agreement. However, the benefits include a funeral purchased according to today's price but delivered in the future when it may cost more. You and your inheritors should weigh the value of investing the money in a funeral versus an account.

Some states have laws to ensure that funds are available to pay for the funeral when required and some require the funeral home or cemetery to invest the funds in a state regulated trust or to purchase a life insurance policy. You should check whether your payment would be invested for your benefit or for the funeral home or cemetery's profit. You should also check what would happen to your prepayment if the funeral home goes out of business and whether you could obtain a refund if you changed your mind or moved away and wished to be buried elsewhere. Some plans can be transferred but may require extra costs. Most of all, you should inform family members or your attorney of the arrangements you have made so that they can carry out your wishes.

Most of all, you should inform family members or your attorney of the arrangements you have made so that they can carry out your wishes.

Chapter Six

FUNERAL DIRECTORS AND OTHER PRACTICALITIES

As we have seen in earlier chapters, making decisions after someone has died is unlike making decisions at other points in our lives. After most deaths, decisions have to be made quickly, and there is little time for reflection and consideration. However, as we have noted, a good deal of thinking through the practicalities and of planning can be done before actions are necessary. After someone dies you often hear phrases such as, "I just want to get the funeral over with," or a little later, "I felt as if I were in limbo until we got through the funeral." Behind such statements there is a recognition that the practicalities surrounding funerals can hold up the emotional side of death. Often people feel they do not have time to grieve properly while so much paperwork and administration remain.

Often people feel they do not have time to grieve properly while so much paperwork and administration remain.

While many of the practicalities and paperwork surrounding death can be done by most capable individuals, it is easier, swifter, and more convenient to involve professionals to organize things at this time. Recognizing this, most people choose to use the services of a funeral director to assist them through the complexities at such an emotionally fragile time.

IMMEDIATELY AFTER A DEATH

Once a person has died, the body is normally moved to one of three places: a hospital morgue, a funeral home, or a government medical examiner's morgue.

Sometimes the next of kin must decide about an autopsy. This can be a legal and medical minefield. In certain states, for example California, an autopsy is a legal requirement if the person has not recently seen a physician. Sometimes the hospital may insist on doing an autopsy. In a situation where the death is unexpected, the medical examiner must be notified in order to determine whether an autopsy is necessary.

When neither the hospital nor the medical examiner think an autopsy is necessary, the next of kin can still insist on one. The main reason for this course of action would be to detect negligence with a view to litigation. We take the position that a deeply suspicious culture seeking litigious opportunities is undesirable. And generally, we suggest that unless there are grounds to believe that negligence has occurred, a needless autopsy should be avoided. If the person dies in hospital, then the autopsy is generally free. However, if the person dies elsewhere (for example, in a nursing home or at home), then it can be harder to arrange an autopsy and there might be a fee.

Such is the skill of modern medics that even after an autopsy, the body can still be displayed in a casket. It will still look normal. An autopsy does not require disfigurement of the body. Finally, on this topic, it is important to remember that, although preliminary findings might be available shortly after the autopsy, the detailed report will take several months. Bits of tissue will need to be examined underneath a microscope. Given the obvious time involved, do expect to contact the doctor or pathologist yourself for the autopsy results.

Choosing between cremation and burial is another decision. Increasingly Americans opt for cremation, which is significantly cheaper than the traditional burial. Gary Lademan in his recent study *Rest in Peace: A Cultural History of Death and the Funeral Home in Twentieth-Century America* estimates that approximately twenty-five percent of Americans select cremation, with it being especially popular in the Southwest and California. As we have noted elsewhere, many find the cremation option attractive, partly because it is more environmentally friendly and partly because it creates attractive options for the use of ashes. It permits one to scatter them in a place that is significant to the family. If you opt for cremation, you have two options. "Direct cremation" involves cremating the body shortly after death, without embalming. This will preclude any viewing or visitation, although, of course, a memorial service could be held with or without the ashes. For a direct cremation, search for a funeral service that provides transportation of the body and delivery of the ashes. The other option would be the same as a traditional funeral service, except that ultimately the body would be cremated.

Assuming one opts for burial, you will need to choose the type of service you will require from the funeral home director. Jessica Mitford's book *The American Way of Death*, published in 1963, has produced a highly desirable transformation in funeral directing. She was deeply critical of the industry and argued that it was highly exploitative. As a result there are now federal and state regulations that require transparency about the costs of services, including those that are required legally, and the full range of casket prices. This Funeral Rule, enforced by the Federal Trade Commission, requires transparency both over the phone and in person.

The Funeral Rule, enforced by the Federal Trade Commission, requires transparency both over the phone and in person.

On caskets, one should be especially careful. Do keep in mind that ultimately the body will "return to dust" and therefore the loved one who has moved on will not be able to appreciate the deluxe model of copper casket, with the delightful mattress, surrounded by satin lace and various liners to protect the body. There are plenty of cheaper models that are equally effective.

Next consider embalming. Over the course of the twentieth century, American attitudes to embalming consciously changed. At the turn of the century there was still some hostility to embalming because it was presumed that the procedure would be disrespectful and perhaps grisly. However, between 1900 and 1920 institutions that trained embalmers proliferated, and gradually this became a key feature of the American funeral.

When they hear the term embalming, many people think of a process similar to that carried out on the mummies of ancient Egypt or on the bodies of Communist rulers. In fact embalming simply means draining the blood from the veins and arteries of the body and replacing this with a preserving fluid (usually some kind of formaldehyde). The process temporarily delays the decomposition of the body by a few days and allows mourners to view the body before the funeral without the shock of seeing the person looking utterly different from how they appeared in life. The body will definitely need to be embalmed if it is to be moved out of state.

Sometimes the impression is given that embalming is a legal requirement. This is *not* the case. You can choose a "direct burial" so that the body is buried shortly after death in a simple container. The main reason embalming is popular is that it helps with the grieving process. Most funeral homes provide visiting hours, when family and friends can view their loved one and say their quiet farewells. This furnishes an opportunity to confront the loved one's departure, and the reality thereby assists the grieving process.

It is worth noting that elsewhere in the western world there is some opposition to the embalming process, mainly on environmental grounds. Embalming fluid is highly toxic, and many feel unhappy about the thought of pints of these chemicals going into the ground at burial or, at the very least, being released into the atmosphere. However, given how common it is to display the body, it looks as if embalming will continue to be a major feature of the American funeral.

Elsewhere in the western world there is some opposition to the embalming process, mainly on environmental grounds.

As we noted earlier, choosing a funeral home is often done at a time of distress and urgency. Although in most states one has the legal option for the family to bury their loved one, most people value the help and support that a funeral home can provide. For this reason the client (funeral home directors *are* businesspeople) is little inclined to be as choosy or as thorough over this financial transaction as usual. When buying a major item such as a car, or even a smaller item such as clothing, we look at the product, compare it with other similar items, and weigh its value for cost. In choosing a funeral home director, however, we act with less care. Our choice may be confined to the funeral homes best known to our immediate community. Recognizing this, the funeral industry provides for the prepaid funerals that we discussed in chapter 5. In addition, some people visit a number of funeral home directors and receive itemized quotations for the type of funeral they desire. In such quotations, full price lists will be given both for the fees (paid to doctors, crematorium, minister, etc.) and for the funeral director's own services (removal of body, coffin, cars, etc.). Whether a funeral director is chosen before or after the death, the Funeral Rule requires that an itemized breakdown of costs be given to the client.

CHOOSING A PLACE AND TIME FOR THE FUNERAL

While the precise timing of the vast majority of funerals is arranged after death, there are a number of decisions that can be made beforehand. Many people have an attachment to a particular church or chapel and wish their funerals to be held there. All churches have different rules and regulations. More details of this and related matters are discussed in chapter 7.

Throughout this book we have encouraged our readers to think through some of the practicalities and decisions of their own funerals. Taking time to visit a church, chapel or funeral home where the funeral might be held is important. Think about issues such as your emotional attachment to the place, its aesthetics, the practicalities of holding a funeral there (a funeral with two hundred mourners, for example, is not easily held in a church in the middle of a field miles from anywhere), and the journey times to the place. It may also be helpful to talk to those who work at the place in which you wish your funeral to be held. The minister of a church, a chaplain of the chapel, and the funeral home staff will all be able to explain what is and is not possible at a particular funeral venue, and this may help you decide if the place is suitable for your needs. Of course, timing is a crucial factor.

FORM OF SERVICE

The range of practical choices regarding the funeral service is huge. In addition to choices already mentioned, such as venue and burial versus cremation, there is great scope for personalizing a service through music, readings, and prayers. Chapter 7 is devoted to the type and shape of funeral services, and chapter 8 covers the music, readings, and prayers that are possible at a funeral service.

ORGAN DONATION

Organ donation has been one of the great successes of the last fifty years in medical research. Nevertheless its widespread use as a medical procedure has been restricted by the relatively small number of people willing to donate their organs after their own death for the use of others. It is now commonplace for the following organs to be donated: skin, liver, heart, heart valves, pancreas, and kidneys. In addition, each year thousands of people benefit from a cornea transplant. It is helpful if organ donation is arranged in advance. However, this can be done at the time of death and tissue donation can be arranged even hours after the death.

MEDICAL RESEARCH

In order to train future doctors and other health-care professionals in their work, hundreds of bodies are needed each year for use in medical education and research. Therefore you might want to think about one of the many "willed body" programs that are found at almost all the major medical schools.

Most of these programs are regulated by state law. If you decide to will your body to medical science, then it is important to inform your next of kin. Once you die, there is, in most cases, a twenty-four-hour phone number that should be called. The school will then make arrangements for the collection of the body. Once the program has finished with the body, the school will cremate the body.

Naturally, bodies that are being donated to medical research must not be embalmed. And of course, it is important that the cause of death was not a communicable disease, such as AIDS, hepatitis, active tuberculosis, or Jakob-Creutzfeldt disease.

The other option is to inform your next of kin that you would be happy to donate your body to a medical school. They will have the power to make that decision at the time of your death. Such would save your immediate family the cost of a funeral. However, if you are thinking of taking this course of action, then you should also consider what service, if any, you wish to be held around the time of your death. Since it is not possible to hold a funeral (because there is no body or coffin on which to focus), many people arrange for a memorial service to be held instead. As with a funeral, the choice of music, readings, and prayers can make this a very special occasion. It gives the mourners a chance to make a formal, and liturgical, goodbye.

FLOWERS AND CHARITY DONATIONS

A choice needs to be made concerning flowers at a funeral. If flowers are wanted, the funeral director should be informed so that proper arrangements can be made. The funeral notice can give the funeral director's address to which flowers may be sent. He or she will then make sure that the flowers are carried to the church or crematorium with the coffin. Flowers can be wreaths arranged by a florist or bouquets or other types of bunches. Once they have arrived, the funeral director will ask if any of the flowers are to be placed on top of the coffin for the funeral service or whether they are simply to be laid out for mourners to see afterwards or taken to the cemetery. You will also need to decide what is to happen to the flowers after the service. Some mourners choose to take at least some of the flowers. Others choose to leave them in the church, cemetery, or crematorium. Still others ask for them to be taken to a local social center. If the flowers are left or taken away, most funeral directors will, as a matter of course, collect the cards that accompany them and give them to the chief mourner.

Some people decide to ask for no flowers at the funeral. Instead they most often wish for the money that would otherwise be spent on the flowers to be given to a charity. Funeral directors will collect this money and pass it on to the charity. While such an intention is laudable, it should also be recognized that some people like to (perhaps, we might say, need to) make a tangible expression of their love and affection for the deceased, and flowers are one way for them to do this.

MONUMENTS AND TOMBSTONES

Decisions concerning a memorial, if any, do not have to be made immediately after death. Nevertheless, it is worth knowing something of the various options. We will consider this in a separate chapter, chapter 9. In the meantime, however, it is enough to say that some funeral directors have stone masons working within their organization while others contract local, independent masons to carry out work on their behalf. Some funeral directors (though these are few) do not deal with memorials or headstones at all.

DEATH NOTICES AND THE OBITUARY

Announcements of death can be made in local and national newspapers in one of two ways. If the person who has died is famous in some way or another, newspapers will often publish an obituary. This does not just give the fact that the person has died but also gives life details and achievements. Most of us, however, will not receive such attention, and mention of the death in the press will have to be paid for. This is called a death notice. The cost of this will depend on the type of newspaper. And in most cases the Funeral Director will organize it for you. In this notice, you can specify whether donations to charity should occur in lieu of flowers.

ASHES

If the deceased has chosen not to be buried, certain decisions will need to be made regarding the cremated remains (ashes) of the deceased. When arrangements for the funeral are being made, the funeral director will ask what the clients would like done with the ashes. Most crematoriums will have the ashes ready for collection on the day following the funeral. Ashes are not normally shipped to the next of kin, but they should be collected personally by them or, for a fee, the funeral director will collect them. Most crematoriums will also hold or store ashes for you if you wish (again, for a fee).

Ashes may be scattered or buried in a cemetery or crematorium grounds or may be taken away by the next of kin or executor of the will to be disposed of elsewhere. There is no law regulating what may or may not be done with cremated remains except that they should be stored or disposed of respectfully. Many funeral homes can arrange for ashes to be buried in a plot in a cemetery or placed in a columbarium or mausoleum. A columbarium is a special room or wall with niches where urns containing cremated remains may be placed and then sealed. Alternatively the ashes could be kept in your home (although, of course, it is important to make arrangements for the ashes once you die) or they could be stored in a church. Both in the grounds of cemeteries and in churchyards there are sometimes family plots where generations of the same family are buried or have their cremated remains placed. It is possible, even with family plots that are centuries old, to have cremated remains interred in a grave that is also a burial plot for coffins.

A columbarium is a special room or wall with niches where urns containing cremated remains may be placed and then sealed.

Some people choose to have their ashes disposed of at sea, and for this no special paperwork is required. People commonly talk of ashes being "scattered" at sea, although this is not what always happens. Care should be taken when committing loose cremated remains to the waves, since sea winds can cause obvious difficulties and embarrassments. As with burial of ashes on land, cremated remains should be contained in something biodegradable. A specially designed urn for use at sea, made of suitable material, but heavy enough to sink quickly to the bottom of the sea where it allows the ashes to disperse, is available. Appropriately it is called a "Neptune urn," and most funeral directors should be able to obtain one for you or give you details of where you may obtain one personally.

COSTS

Funerals are not cheap. According to the 1995 NFDA (National Funeral Directors Association) Survey of Funeral Home Operations, the charge for an adult, full-service funeral in 1990 was $4,624. This charge included the following services:

- a professional service charge
- transfer of remains
- embalming
- use of viewing facilities
- use of facilities for ceremony
- hearse
- limousine
- 18-gauge steel casket with a velvet interior

Vault, cemetery, and monument charges were not included, so it is easy to spend up to $10,000.

It is worth remembering that there may be some help with these charges. Social Security and veterans' benefits might be available. Free burials are available to veterans within a national cemetery and with a grave marker. Naturally the family will have to pay for any services beyond this basic provision. At the end of the book you will find details of memorial societies, which are private associations that encourage members to explore low-cost funerals.

Perhaps the most important advice we can recommend is for both the person dying and the close family to face these practical questions together.

Perhaps the most important advice we can recommend is for both the person dying and the close family to face these practical questions together. This can be an opportunity for prayer and mutual support and might open up necessary conversations such as "please don't invite Cousin John." And it allows you to create together that most paradoxical of occasions, the good funeral.

✍ Chapter Seven
FUNERAL SERVICES

We noted earlier that there is a basic human need to mark the end of life with some ritual or ceremony. Over the thousands of years of human history and today throughout the world, the forms that funerals take are many and varied. When thinking about what should take place at a funeral service, truth is, whatever works. What, then, is it that a funeral is meant to achieve? What is its purpose?

Each funeral's purpose is unique since a different set of circumstances leads up to it and a different set of needs must be met for those who attend it. In America in the twenty-first century, however, a Christian funeral might be characterized by:

- giving thanks for a life
- commending the deceased to God
- expressing grief
- showing the love of God, found in the life of Jesus, to the bereaved
- pausing to think of human mortality
- saying farewell
- disposing of the body

For many previous generations in America, funerals took place in the town in which the person was born, lived, and died. Today people rarely live their whole lives in one place, and any church to which they might have an attachment (perhaps through marriage or other family reasons) may not be the church nearest to where they die. This will mean that often both the minister of the church and the family are getting to know each other through the process of arranging and organizing a funeral.

The particular use of a church to mark the transition from this life to the "life to come" can help Christians comprehend that transition.

In this chapter we will explore the church funeral. The particular use of a church to mark the transition from this life to the "life to come" can help Christians comprehend that transition much more effectively than a simple graveside committal service. At the end of this chapter we also say something briefly about memorial services.

FUNERALS IN CHURCH

The basic structure of most Christian funeral services in America today is broadly the same. While the liturgies of a small number of funerals reflect ceremonies of the Orthodox Church and the Society of Friends (Quakers), most contain:

- gathering
- readings and sermon
- prayers

- commendation and farewell
- committal
- dismissal

Gathering

Because a funeral service is an act of Christian worship, it should be approached and prepared for appropriately. What is considered appropriate will differ according to individual circumstances. There is, for instance, an ancient tradition of the coffin being received into the church the night before the funeral takes place. Though this is by no means customary today, where it does occur the coffin may be sprinkled with water, as a reminder of our shared baptism, and prayers may be said, as it comes through the church door. As a further symbol of the Christian faith into which the deceased had been baptized, the lit Easter (paschal) candle is often placed near the coffin, reminding the congregation of Christ's presence among them and of his victory over death. For the same purpose a pall, a simple white cloth, is sometimes placed over the coffin, often by family and friends of the deceased.

Whenever the coffin does arrive and the congregation is in church, the minister says an opening prayer and then an opening hymn may be sung. Any planned tributes by family members or friends follow. If desired, prayers of penitence may then be said. These prayers can be very useful to the mourners since most of us have something to regret in our dealings with every person we know. Prayers at this point in the service therefore serve as a chance to wipe the slate clean and receive the assurance of God's forgiveness before we continue with our farewell to the departed. The gathering section finishes with a special prayer called the collect, in which the minister "collects" up the thoughts of the whole congregation about those who have died generally and the deceased person in particular.

Readings and Sermon

For this section there should be at least one reading from the Bible and, if desired, multiple readings from either the Bible or an appropriate piece of poetry or other literature. If a reading from a non-biblical source is used, it is also possible to place this reading toward the end of the service, probably after the prayers. Both these kinds of readings give the chance for a friend or relative of the deceased to be involved in the service. If you are planning your own funeral, it is important that you ask the people you have in mind if they would be happy to assist in this way. If they are not asked but simply told after death (by instructions in the will or by other written means), it may be very difficult for them to say no to the request, even if they do not feel comfortable saying yes.

Not only does the sermon explicitly proclaim the Christian content of the service, but it is also where the minister talks in a personal way about the deceased.

The sermon at funerals has an especially important part to play. Not only does it explicitly proclaim the Christian content of the service, but it is also the point where the minister talks in a personal way about the deceased. In this manner the minister speaks both for the church and for the bereaved. To do this well and enable the congregation to feel that the words they have heard have spoken for them and reflect their own, varied experiences of the deceased is a skillful art. In writing funeral sermons, many clergy are appreciative of any written material about the deceased that they can read to help prepare them. Increasingly, many church people who are planning their own funerals take time to write out a brief biography and to highlight some of the things in their lives that have been most important to them. Sermons at funerals are almost always preached by members of the clergy or other licensed preachers. If another spoken, personal remembrance is desired, to be delivered by either a family member or friend, it might be best placed at the end of the gathering section.

Prayers

Prayers are usually led by the minister who conducts the service, but it is perfectly possible for another person, not necessarily ordained, to lead them. Although the individual circumstances of the situation and the needs of the congregation should determine what kinds of prayers are said, it is usual that the following pattern is observed:

- thanksgiving for the life of the departed
- prayer for those who mourn
- prayers of penitence (if not already used)
- prayer for readiness to live in the light of eternity

It is also appropriate for the prayers to be more than a set of words to which all respond "amen" and may include spontaneous petitions with fuller responses by the congregation. These prayers are usually followed by the Our Father (Lord's Prayer), unless that prayer is reserved for later in the service as part of the dismissal.

Commendation and Farewell

The commendation is a further prayer in which the deceased person is entrusted to God's merciful keeping. The minister who is leading the service says this prayer while standing near the coffin. If the service is attended by a small number of people, it may be appropriate to ask those at the service to gather round the coffin at this point. Many Roman Catholic and Anglican funerals also insert the ceremony of sprinkling the coffin with water at this stage of the service. Like the sprinkling at the beginning of the service, this action recalls the water of baptism and can be performed by all those attending and not just the minister who is presiding. At this point in the service, some clergy also encourage the censing of the coffin with incense. The incense symbolizes the prayers of the congregation rising up to God.

Committal

The committal is the final prayer over the coffin before the body goes to its resting place. Variously this might be immediately prior to lowering the casket into the grave, as the coffin is removed from church to be taken to the crematorium, or, if already at the crematorium, as it is consigned to the flames. If the committal takes place at the graveside, some clergy bless the grave with a short prayer and, after the coffin has been lowered into place, perhaps also sprinkle it with water and cense it. After the prayer of committal at the graveside, earth is scattered on the coffin, both by the minister and by members of the immediate family. At many funerals it is increasingly common for all those present to throw a handful of earth into the grave. This acts as another physical gesture demonstrating their acceptance of the death and their participation in committing the loved one to his or her final resting place.

Dismissal

The final part of a funeral liturgy is the dismissal. There is no set form of words for this, and the minister leading the service may say such prayers as he or she deems appropriate for the occasion. These might include the Our Father, the Nunc Dimittis (Luke 2:29–32), or perhaps a simple prayer of blessing over the congregation. The minister might lead the congregation in singing a prayer of dismissal.

The Eucharist

Most funerals that take place in America today do not involve a communion service (also known as the Eucharist, the Mass, or the Lord's Supper). Many Christians, however, plan for their own funeral to take place within such a context. Every Eucharist celebrates the life, death, and resurrection of Jesus, and it is therefore most appropriate that a funeral service, which celebrates the new life brought to every Christian believer, brings these two together. When the Eucharist is to be celebrated as part of the funeral it takes place between the prayers and the commendation and farewell.

Chapter 8 in this book, on the music, readings, and prayers, gives suggestions applicable to a funeral within the Eucharist. When planning a funeral service involving communion, the religious faith, or otherwise, of the mourners should be taken into account. It might not be appropriate to celebrate the Eucharist, for instance, if most of the mourners are not churchgoers, as they may feel alienated and removed from the service when the congregation is invited to receive the bread and wine. In such circumstances some have suggested that it might be better for the coffin to be brought into church the night before the funeral and for the Eucharist to be celebrated that evening or the following morning before the funeral.

MEMORIAL SERVICES

A memorial service is a relatively modern phenomenon both in America and more generally in the Western world. The first memorial service in America was probably held in Illinois at Woodlawn Cemetery in Jackson County on April 29, 1866, to honor those who had died in the Civil War. Before that, there were memorial services in England after the death of Princess Charlotte, the twenty-year-old only child of George IV (and therefore heir to the throne) in 1817. The widespread national mourning felt throughout Britain was replicated in 1852 when memorial services were held throughout the country to coincide with the funeral of the Duke of Wellington in St. Paul's Cathedral. Nine years later similar services remembered the life of Prince Albert, Queen Victoria's husband.

Rarely, however, do memorial services meet a need if they are held too long after the death.

Today there may be a variety of reasons for considering a memorial service. Most memorial services are held in a church. A memorial service might be arranged in addition to a funeral if the funeral was far away from many of the mourners. For instance, a person might have died in Texas but until recently lived in Maine, and friends there also want to remember her. A memorial service might be held if the church or chapel where the funeral took place was too small to accommodate all those who wanted to attend (this may be the case when a public figure or a young person dies). Those who give their bodies for medical education and research might choose a memorial service since the body will be removed to the medical school and there is no possibility of a funeral.

Memorial services can provide for these and other contingencies. Rarely, however, do memorial services meet a need if they are held too long after the death (say, more than two months). This is because, like funerals, memorial services are part of the grieving process. If the memorial service is unduly delayed the service may not meet the needs of the congregation in such an obvious or helpful way. If it is to be held much later, then the readings, prayers, music, and sermon should all reflect the fact that the grief of the mourners has moved on and is almost certainly not felt as sharply as it was immediately after the death.

THE WAKE

In many countries of the world the mourners at a funeral will gather together before the service to remember the loved one who has died. This vigil often begins at the time the coffin is received into church the night before the funeral and continues through the following day. For this reason it may be called a "wake," since those gathered are staying awake until the service itself. At such a gathering, people talk privately or publicly about the deceased as they share their memories, mourn the person's passing, and receive the love and support of the Christian community that has come together. The wake takes place most often in the home of the deceased or in the home of a close relative. In America today wakes are still popular, and many funerals invite the guests back after the service for a similar gathering.

Chapter Eight

MUSIC, READINGS, AND PRAYERS

T hus far this book has been concerned largely with the practicalities of legal, financial, and logistical matters. All this is vital, of course, in ensuring that what happens after death is what was intended by the person who died. We have looked at the settings for a funeral service and at the order that such a service may take. We have seen that a large part of a funeral service is prescribed by the various Christian denominations (though we saw, too, that there was scope for adaptation) and that certain elements are regarded as essential when putting together a funeral liturgy. However, this book is a funeral handbook, and it is to suggestions for the content of the funeral service itself that we now turn. There is much in the service that can be chosen and personalized by either the person whose funeral it is or those arranging the funeral. All this is best done in consultation with the priest or minister who will lead the service.

There is much in the service that can be chosen and personalized by either the person whose funeral it is or those arranging the funeral.

Through the choice of music, readings, and prayers, the mood of the service can be set and certain themes can be emphasized. The funeral service itself is probably the one and only chance for certain things to be said and given prominence in the whole of the bereavement process. It is almost certain that only at the funeral will family and friends of the deceased be gathered together in one place at the same time. Through advanced choice of music, readings, and prayers, the deceased person can share with all those gathered exactly what the tone of remembrance might be. For instance one person, in planning his own funeral, created an opportunity both for reflection on the shortness of human life and for a smile by choosing the song "Je ne regrette rien" as part of his service. Appropriate use of music, readings, and prayers also allows certain family members and friends of the deceased to take an active part in the service either by reading aloud or leading the prayers. Some people are also lucky enough to have friends who are musically accomplished and who would be delighted to be asked to use their talents during the service. Organists, singers, and other musicians can all participate in such a way if desired.

MUSIC

There are a numbers of points during a funeral service when music is appropriate. This may be either organ music, music played on other instruments, hymns sung by all the members of congregation, or perhaps music sung by a choir or a soloist. Music may be performed before, during, and after the service. Organ music can be played before the service starts while the congregation assembles and at the end of the service as people depart (though most organists would prefer the congregation to remain seated and to listen to the music that they have spent time practicing). It is also quite common for there to be special music at other points in the service. This may be an anthem sung by a choir, a piece played by a soloist or a group, or recorded music played from a CD or tape. The latter is increasingly popular.

Processional

The music at the beginning of a service can play a crucial role in setting the tone for the rest of the funeral. Depending on the feeling that you want the funeral to convey, quiet or loud, serious or light music might variously be appropriate. During the actual service (as it begins in fact), people often choose to play music as the coffin is carried into church, preceded by the minister. The following pieces of music, many for organ, express a whole range of modes and feelings. Many might well also be played at the end of the service. Some of the pieces were written for orchestra or strings but can be found in adaptations for organ. As with music before the service, some of these pieces will most easily be played on CD or tape.

Special music may be an anthem sung by a choir, a piece played by a soloist or a group, or recorded music played from a CD or tape.

- Albinoni—Adagio in G Minor
- J. S. Bach—Cantata no. 208, no. 9, Schafe konnen sicher weiden (Sheep May Safely Graze)
- J. S. Bach—Cantata no. 147, no. 10, Jesu bleibet meine Freude (Jesu, Joy of Man's Desiring)
- J. S. Bach—Toccata and Fugue in D Minor
- Barber—Adagio for Strings
- Beethoven—Piano Concerto no. 4, first movement
- Beethoven—Symphony no. 6, last movement
- Beethoven—Violin Concerto in D Minor, second movement
- Brahms—Symphony no. 3, last movement
- Britten—Simple Symphony, third movement, Sentimental Sarabande
- Chopin—Nocturne no. 8 in D-flat
- Chopin—Prelude no. 4 in E Minor
- Chopin—Sonata no. 2 in B-flat Minor, Funeral Sonata
- Copland—Fanfare for the Common Man
- Debussy—Suite Bergamasque, no. 3, Clair de lune
- Debussy—Prelude no. 8, La fille aux cheveux de lin (The Girl with the Flaxen Hair)
- Delius—A Village Romeo and Juliet, no. 19, The Walk to the Paradise Garden
- Dvorak—Symphony no. 9, From the New World, second movement (Going Home)

- Elgar—Variations on an Original Theme, Enigma, no. 9, Nimrod
- Elgar—Serenade, second movement
- Elgar—Symphony no. 1, first movement
- Elgar—Symphony no. 2, slow movement
- Grieg—Holberg Suite, no. 4, Air
- Grieg—Two Elegiac Melodies, no. 2, Last Spring
- Handel—Water Music, no. 1f, Air
- Haydn—The Seven Last Words of Our Saviour on the Cross
- Haydn—String Quartet, Op. 76, no. 3 in C, Emperor, second movement
- Holst—The Planets, no. 4, Jupiter
- Karg-Elert—Choral Improvisations, no. 59, Nun danket alle Gott
- MacDowell—Woodland Sketches, no. 1, To a Wild Rose
- Mahler—Symphony no. 5, Adagietto, Death in Venice
- Messaien—L'Ascension
- Mozart—Piano Concerto no. 21 in C, second movement (Elvira Madigan)
- Puccini—Preludio sinfonico
- Ravel—Pavane pour une infante défunte
- Schoenberg—Verklarte Nacht
- Schubert—String Quartet no. 14 in D Minor, Death and the Maiden, second movement
- Schubert—Piano Sonata no. 21 in B-flat, second movement

- Schubert—String Quintet in C, first and second movements
- Schubert—Impromptu no. 3 in G-flat
- Schubert—Impromptu no. 4 in A-flat
- Strauss—Vier letzte lieder, no. 4, Im abendrot (At Sunset)
- Strauss—Metamorphosen
- Tavener—The Protecting Veil, opening
- Vaughan Williams—Fantasia on a Theme of Thomas Tallis
- Vaughan Williams—The Lark Ascending
- Wagner—Tristan und Isolde, no. 19, Liebestod (Death in Love)
- Wagner—Gotterdammerung, no. 37 (Siegfried's Funeral March)
- Widor—Symphony no. 5, Toccata

Hymns

There are a number of hymns especially written with funeral services in mind and plenty of other general hymns that are well suited to the occasion. You might like to choose your favorite hymns or those that have special associations. For instance, some people select hymns for the funeral that were sung at their wedding or at the funeral of their partner. Why not ask your minister if you can borrow a hymnbook from church in order to look at the words of various hymns to help you in your choice? When choosing hymns, remember that newer or less frequently sung hymns might not be known by those attending the service and thus might result in the singing at the funeral being less than hearty!

Listed below are some funeral hymns and other tried and tested popular hymns for funerals.

Hymns written specifically for funerals:

- Brief Life Is Here Our Portion
- Christ, Enthroned in Highest Heaven
- Day of Wrath! O Day of Mourning!
- God Be in My Head
- Jesus, Son of Mary
- Now the Evening Shadows Closing
- Now the Laborer's Task Is O'er
- O Lord, to Whom the Spirits Live
- What Sweet of Life Endureth

General hymns also suitable for funerals:

- Abide with Me; Fast Falls the Eventide
- All Things Bright and Beautiful
- As Pants the Hart for Cooling Streams
- Blest Are the Pure in Heart
- Guide Me, O Thou Great Redeemer
- He Wants Not Friends That Hath Thy Love
- I Danced in the Morning
- Jerusalem the Golden
- Jesus Lives! Thy Terrors Now
- Joy and Triumph Everlasting
- Let Saints on Earth in Concert Sing
- Lord, It Belongs Not to My Care

- Now Is Eternal Life
- Now Thank We All Our God
- O God, Our Help in Ages Past
- Praise, My Soul, the King of Heaven
- Praise to the Holiest in the Height
- The Day Thou Gavest, Lord, Is Ended
- The King of Love My Shepherd Is
- The Lord's My Shepherd, I'll Not Want
- There Is a Land of Pure Delight
- They Whose Course on Earth Is O'er
- Thine Be the Glory, Risen, Conquering Son

Psalms

If the funeral is to include a celebration of Holy Communion, you have an opportunity to choose a psalm to be sung. Usually a psalm (or sometimes another hymn) is sung immediately before the reading of the Gospel or between the first and second readings. It can be sung either by the whole congregation or by a choir. To help you make your choice, look at a Bible or a Psalter (a book of psalms, set to music). The following are offered as suggestions for you to consider.

- Psalm 23 (The LORD is my shepherd.)
- Psalm 25:6–7, 17–18, 20–21 (Be mindful of your mercy, O LORD.)
- Psalm 27:1, 4, 7–9, 13–14 (The LORD is my light.)
- Psalm 42:2–3, 5 (My soul thirsts for God.)
- Psalm 62:2–6, 8–9 (He alone is my rock.)

- Psalm 103:8, 10, 13–18 (The LORD is merciful.)
- Psalm 115:1, 9–13 (Not to us, O LORD, not to us.)
- Psalm 116:10–11, 15–16 (I kept my faith.)
- Psalm 130 (Out of the depths I cry.)
- Psalm 143:1–2, 5–8, 10 (Hear my prayer, O LORD.)

Anthems

There is a wide range of choral music that may be sung as an anthem in a funeral service. The possibilities are really restricted only by the appropriateness of the music to a funeral service. Here again consultation with the officiating minister is of great importance. Having an anthem allows for certain thoughts and feelings to be expressed by the person who chooses the music in a way which is not possible with instrumental music. With anthems it is not only the tone of music that is conveyed but also a message through the words. The anthem is also likely to be listened to more attentively than processional and recessional music. This is because music at these points occurs when attenders are likely to be looking at the coffin being brought into or out of church, and they may be feeling more emotional at these points. Remember, too, that not everyone will remain in church at the end of a funeral to hear the whole piece of music played, and they may not have been at church early enough to hear all of the music played

With anthems it is not only the tone of music that is conveyed but also a message through the words.

before the service either. Some possible anthems to choose from include:

- Anerio—Missa pro Defunctis, Kyrie, and Sanctus
- Bainton—And I Saw a New Heaven
- Bairstow—Jesu, Grant Me This I Pray
- Bairstow—Save Us, O Lord
- Byrd—Ave Verum Corpus
- Byrd—Four-Part Mass, Agnus Dei
- Byrd—Gradualia Vol. 1, Iustorum Animae
- Byrd—Short Service, Nunc Dimittis
- Croft—Funeral Sentences, Burial Service
- Elgar—Ave Verum Corpus
- Gibbons—Almighty and Everlasting God
- Gibbons—First (Short) Service, Nunc Dimittis
- Goss—O Saviour of the World
- Goss—O Taste and See How Gracious the Lord Is
- Harris—Bring Us, O Lord God
- Harris—Evening Hymn
- Harris—Fair Is the Heaven
- Howells—Take Him, Earth, for Cherishing
- Ireland—Greater Love Hath No Man Than This
- Morley—Short Service, Nunc Dimittis
- Mozart—Ave Verum Corpus
- Palestrina—Missa Brevis, Agnus Dei
- Parry—Songs of Farewell
- Parsons—Ave Maria

- Phillips—Christ in Five Parts, Ave Verum Corpus
- Rutter—God Be in My Head
- Stainer—The Crucifixion, no. 5, God So Loved the World
- Stanford—Services in B-flat, Nunc Dimittis
- Stanford—Three Motets, no. 1, Justorum Animae
- Stanford—Three Motets, no. 3, Beati Quorum Via
- Tallis—If Ye Love Me, Keep My Commandments
- Tavener—Funeral Ikos
- Tomkins—Third Service, Nunc Dimittis
- Walford Davies—God Be in My Head
- Walford Davies—Solemn Melody
- Walmisley—Evening Service in D Minor, Nunc Dimittis
- Walton—Drop, Drop Slow Tears
- Walton—Where Does the Uttered Music Go?
- S. S. Wesley—Let Us Lift Up Our Hearts
- S. S. Wesley—Man That Is Born of Woman
- S. S. Wesley—Thou Wilt Keep Him in Perfect Peace

Recessional Music

Like the music played before the service, the music at the end can have an important part for the grieving mourners. Some people will want quiet, unobtrusive music played both before and after the service, while others might choose a more upbeat piece of music on which to end the service, expressing the Christian belief in the resurrection. A wide range of music for the end of the service is therefore possible. The choices here are similar to those for the processional music and therefore no separate list is necessary.

Other Music

Although most music that is played or sung in church funeral services is live, much of the music at crematorium funerals is now played on a sound system from a CD or tape. It is possible, too, for such music to be used in church. Music played in this way has become popular for a number of reasons. Perhaps an organist or choir is not always available. Perhaps it is impractical for reasons of cost, size of church, etc., to have certain pieces of music performed live. For instance, your church and your wallet may not be able to accommodate the London Symphony Orchestra! Music from CD or tape also has the advantage of guaranteeing a certain level of performance. This recorded music may be appropriate at any of the various points discussed earlier in this chapter. As with more "traditional" music, it is always best to arrange the music in consultation with and at the discretion of the minister. The list of possible recorded pieces is almost endless, and it might be overtly religious or secular. As music from the former category has been discussed and suggested

As with more "traditional" music, it is always best to arrange the music in consultation with and at the discretion of the minister.

above and music from the latter category is highly personal, it is not necessary to provide a list of suggestions at this point. The positive reaction to the music at the funeral of Diana, Princess of Wales, which included songs such as Elton John's "Candle in the Wind," illustrates the increasing acceptance and popularity of secular music.

READINGS FROM SCRIPTURE

As we saw in chapter 7, there is scope for one or more Bible readings at a funeral service. In the section below we offer some suggestions. Each Bible reference is followed by a very brief description of the passage's topic. It is a good idea to get a copy of a modern translation of the Bible and read through the passages. Some will appeal more than others. This is fine. Choose the reading(s) that most reflect what you feel about the Christian faith and its hope and that you want to share with others at the funeral. You might like to look at more than one translation of a passage as they often convey different nuances or emphases. We suggest that you begin by consulting the New Revised Standard Version.

Choose the reading(s) that most reflect what you feel about the Christian faith and its hope and that you want to share with others at the funeral.

Old Testament and Apocrypha

- Genesis 42:29–38 (The sorrow you would cause would kill me.)
- 2 Samuel 1:17, 23–26 (David laments for Saul and Jonathan.)

- 2 Samuel 12:16–23 (David's son dies.)
- Job 19:1, 23–27 (This I know: my Redeemer lives.)
- Isaiah 25:6–9 (The Lord will destroy death for ever.)
- Isaiah 53:1–10 (The suffering servant is described.)
- Isaiah 61:1–3 (Comfort all those who mourn.)
- Lamentations 3:17–26 (Wait in silence, for the love of the Lord never comes to an end.)
- Daniel 12:1–3, 5–9 (Those who lie sleeping in the dust will awake, for their names are written in the book.)
- Wisdom 3:1–9 (The souls of the righteous are in the hands of God.)
- Wisdom 4:7–15 (Age is not length of time, but an untarnished life.)
- Ecclesiasticus 38:16–23 (Do not forget that there is no coming back.)
- 2 Maccabees 12:43–45 (He took account of the resurrection in a fine and noble action.)

Psalms

- Psalm 6 (O LORD, do not rebuke me.)
- Psalm 23 (The LORD is my shepherd.)
- Psalm 25 (To you, O LORD, I lift up my soul.)
- Psalm 27 (The LORD is my light.)
- Psalm 32 (Happy are those whose transgression is forgiven.)

- Psalm 38:9–22 (O LORD, all my longing is known to you.)
- Psalm 39 (I will guard my ways.)
- Psalm 42 (As a deer longs for flowing streams.)
- Psalm 90 (Lord, you have been our dwelling place.)
- Psalm 116 (I love the LORD.)
- Psalm 118:4–29 (His steadfast love endures forever.)
- Psalm 120 (In my distress I cry to the LORD.)
- Psalm 121 (I lift up my eyes to the hills.)
- Psalm 130 (Out of the depths I cry to you, O LORD.)
- Psalm 138 (I give you thanks, O LORD.)
- Psalm 139 (O LORD, you have searched me.)

New Testament

- Romans 5:6–11 (Having died to make us righteous, is it likely that Christ would now fail to save us from God's anger?)
- Romans 5:17–21 (However great the number of sins committed, grace is even greater.)
- Romans 6:3–9 (All those who have been baptized into Jesus Christ were baptized into his death.)
- Romans 8:14–23 (We wait for our bodies to be set free.)
- Romans 8:31–39 (Nothing can come between us and the love of God.)

- Romans 14:7–12 (Whether we are living or dead, we belong to the Lord.)
- 1 Corinthians 15:20–23 (All will be brought to life in Christ.)
- 1 Corinthians 15:20–58 (Death is swallowed up in victory—the resurrection of the dead.)
- 2 Corinthians 4:7–15 (We carry in our mortal bodies the death of Jesus.)
- 2 Corinthians 4:16–5:10 (Visible things last only for a while, but the invisible is eternal.)
- 2 Corinthians 5:1, 6–10 (We have an everlasting home in heaven.)
- Ephesians 3:14–21 (We have the power to understand Christ's love.)
- Philippians 3:10–21 (God's purpose for all of us is that we will be transformed.)
- 1 Thessalonians 4:13–18 (We shall always be with the Lord.)
- 2 Timothy 2:8–13 (If we have died with him, we shall also live with him.)
- 1 Peter 1:3–9 (We have been born anew to a living hope.)
- 1 John 3:1–3 (We shall see him as he really is and shall be like him.)
- 1 John 3:14–16 (We have passed out of death and into life because we love those around us.)
- Revelation 7:9–17 (The crowd worships in heaven.)
- Revelation 21:1–7 (Behold, I make all things new.)

- Revelation 21:22–27; 22:3b–5 (The Lord God will be their light.)

Gospel Readings

- Matthew 5:1–12 (Rejoice and be glad for your reward will be great in heaven.)
- Matthew 11:25–30 (Come to me, and I will give you rest.)
- Matthew 25:31–46 (Come, you whom the Father has blessed.)
- Mark 10:13–16 (Let the little children come to me.)
- Mark 15:33–39; 16:1–6 (He has risen; he is not here.)
- Luke 7:11–17 (Young man, I tell you to get up.)
- Luke 12:35–40 (The Son of Man is coming. Stand ready.)
- Luke 23:33, 39–43 (Today you will be with me in paradise.)
- Luke 24:1–11 (The resurrection is described.)
- Luke 24:13–35 (Was it not ordained that Christ should suffer and enter into his glory?)
- John 5:19–29 (Whoever hears my word and believes him who sent me has eternal life.)
- John 6:35–40 (Whoever believes in the Son has eternal life, and I shall raise him up on the last day.)

- John 6:51–58 (Anyone who eats this bread has eternal life, and I shall raise him up at the last day.)
- John 11:17–27 (I am the resurrection and the life.)
- John 11:32–45 (Lazarus is raised from the dead.)
- John 12:23–28 (If a grain of wheat dies, it yields a rich harvest.)
- John 14:1–6 (There are many rooms in my Father's house.)
- John 17:24–26 (I want them to be where I am.)
- John 19:17–18, 25b–30 (Bowing his head, he gave up his spirit.)
- John 19:38–42 (Christ is buried.)
- John 20:1–10 (Christ is raised from the dead.)

OTHER READINGS

As well as having a reading or two from the Bible, it may be that there is a particular piece of prose or a poem that could also be read at the funeral. Those planning their own funerals might want to share a favorite piece of literature with their family and friends. Those who are organizing the funeral of another person might want to read from something other than the Bible to offer words of comfort. Whatever the reason for choosing such a piece, as with all other parts of the funeral, it is important that the reading reflects something of the deceased or is directed toward the needs of the mourners. We offer the following four readings in full—the first is often used at funerals—for you to consider as examples of suitable readings for funerals. All four have a theme, the continuing presence of the loved one beyond the grave. They show the variety of poetry and prose that can be used in funerals. Continuing presence is, of course, only one theme, and there are others that you might like to explore including consolation, eternal life, celebration, thanks, reconciliation, faith, hope, and love.

It is important that the reading reflects something of the deceased or is directed toward the needs of the mourners.

"Death Is Nothing at All," Henry Scott Holland

"Death is nothing at all. It does not count. I have only slipped away into the next room. Nothing has happened. Everything remains exactly as it was. I am I, and you are you, and the old life that we lived so fondly together is untouched, unchanged. Whatever we were to each other, that we are still. Call me by the old familiar name. Speak of me in the easy way which you always used. Put no difference into your tone. Wear no forced air of solemnity or sorrow. Laugh as we always laughed at the little jokes that we enjoyed together. Play, smile, think of me, ~~pray for~~ HEBREWS 9:27 ~~me~~. Let my name be ever the household word that it always was. Let it be spoken without an effort, without the ghost of a shadow upon it.

"Life means all that it ever meant. It is the same as it ever was. There is absolute and unbroken continuity. What is this death but a negligible accident? Why should I be out of mind because I am out of sight? I am but waiting for you, for an interval, somewhere very near, just around the corner. All is well. Nothing is hurt; nothing is lost. One brief moment and all will be as it was before. How we shall laugh at the trouble of parting when we meet again!"[1]

"The Ship," Victor Hugo

"I am standing upon that foreshore. A ship at my side spreads her white sails in the morning breeze and starts for the blue ocean. She is an object of beauty and strength and I stand and watch her until at length she hangs like a speck of white cloud just where the sea and sky come down to mingle with each other.

"Then someone at my side says, 'There! She is gone!' 'Gone where?' 'Gone from my sight, that's all.' She is just as large in mast and spar and hull as ever she was when she left my side; just as able to bear her load of living freight to the place of her destination. Her diminished size is in me, not in her. And just at that moment when someone at my side says, 'There! She is gone!' there are other eyes watching her coming and other voices ready to take up the glad shout, 'Here she comes!' And that is dying."[2]

"Remember," Christina Georgina Rossetti

"Remember me when I am gone away,
Gone far away into the silent land;
When you can no more hold me by the hand,

Nor I half turn to go, yet turning stay.
Remember me when no more day by day
You tell me of our future that you plann'd:
Only remember me; you understand
It will be late to counsel then or pray.
Yet if you should forget me for a while
And afterwards remember, do not grieve:
For if the darkness and corruption leave
A vestige of the thoughts that once I had,
Better by far you should forget and smile
Than that you should remember and be sad."[3]

"Music, When Soft Voices Die," Percy Bysshe Shelley

"Music, when soft voices die,
vibrates in the memory;
Odours, when sweet violets sicken,
live within the sense they quicken.

"Rose leaves, when the rose is dead,
are heaped for the beloved's bed;
And so thy thoughts, when thou art gone,
love itself shall slumber on."[4]

PRAYERS

As with the readings, the kinds of prayers that are used at a funeral will help convey the sense in which the deceased person wished to be remembered. There is a world of difference, for instance, between a prayer for someone tragically and unexpectedly killed and a prayer for a person who knew death was coming and had prepared for this. In this final section we suggest some different topics or themes for prayer, which you may consider when planning a funeral. Every funeral is different because every human life is different, but human experience is often very similar. Because of this, one prayer is given for each theme. We hope that the themes listed will help you think about the tone of the funeral you are planning and the suitability, or otherwise, of the different kinds of prayer to be used in the service. Please remember that the pastor, priest, or minister leading the service will have certain prayers which she will want to use. Why not talk to whoever will be taking the service and ask for advice about what would help make a good set of prayers?

Bidding (Opening) Prayer

O Lord, support us all the long days of this troublous life, until the shades lengthen and the evening comes, and the busy world is over and our work is done. Then, Lord, in your mercy, grant us a safe lodging, a holy rest, and peace at the last, through Jesus Christ our Lord. Amen.

Grief

O God of grace and glory, we give you thanks for giving [name] to us to know and love as a companion on our earthly pilgrimage. In your boundless compassion, console all who mourn; give us faith to see in death the gate of eternal life, so that, in quiet confidence we may continue on earth, until by your call, we are united with those who have gone before, through Jesus Christ our Lord. Amen.

Remembrance

Grant, O Lord, that keeping in glad remembrance those who have gone before, who have stood by us and helped us, who have cheered us by their sympathy and strengthened us by their example, we may seize every opportunity of life and rejoice in the promise of a glorious resurrection with them, through Jesus Christ our Lord. Amen.

Thanksgiving

God our Father, we thank you that you have made each one of us in your own image, and given us gifts and talents with which to serve you. We thank you for [name], the joys and trials we shared together, the good we saw in him/her, the love we received from him/her. Now give us strength and courage to leave him/her in your care, confident in your promise of eternal life, through Jesus Christ our Lord. Amen.

Consolation

Father of mercies and God of all consolation, you pursue us with untiring love and dispel the shadow of death with the bright dawn of life. Comfort your family in their loss and sorrow. Be our refuge and our strength, O Lord, and lift us from the depths of grief into the peace and light of your presence. Your Son, our Lord Jesus Christ, by dying has destroyed our death, and by rising, restored our life. Enable us therefore to press on toward him, so that, after our earthly course is run, he may reunite us with those we love, when every tear will be wiped away. We ask this through Christ our Lord. Amen.

Petition

Bring us, O Lord God, at our last awakening into the house and gate of heaven, to enter into that gate, and dwell in that house, where there shall be no darkness or dazzling, but one equal light; no noise or silence, but one equal music; no fears nor hopes, but one equal possession; no ends nor beginnings, but one equal eternity, in the habitation of your glory and dominion, world without end. Amen.

Mercy

Into your hands, O Lord, we humbly entrust our beloved brother/sister [name]. In this life you embraced him/her with your tender love; deliver him/her from every evil and bid him/her enter eternal rest. The old order has passed away. Welcome him/her then into paradise, where there will be no sorrow, no weeping nor pain, but the fullness of peace and joy with your Son and the Holy Spirit for ever and ever. Amen.

Bring us, O Lord God, at our last awakening into the house and gate of heaven.

Penitence

God our Redeemer, you love all that you have made; you are merciful beyond our deserving. Pardon your servants' sins, acknowledged and unperceived. Help us also to forgive as we pray to be forgiven, through him who on the cross asked forgiveness of those who wounded him. Amen.

Peace

Lord, make me a channel of thy peace; where there is hatred may I bring love; where there is injury, pardon; where there is doubt, faith; where there is despair, hope; where there is darkness, light; and where there is sadness, joy. O Divine Master, grant that we may not so much seek to be consoled as to console; to be understood as to understand; to be loved as to love; for it is in giving that we receive, it is in pardoning that we are pardoned, and it is in dying that we are born to eternal life. Amen.

Commendation

Give rest, O Christ, to your servant with thy saints, where sorrow and pain are no more; neither sighing, but life everlasting. You only art immortal, the Creator and Maker of all, and we are mortal, formed of the earth, and unto earth shall we return as you ordained, when you created us saying, "Dust you are, and to dust you shall return." We all go down to the dust, and weeping at the grave we make our song: alleluia, alleluia, alleluia.

Hold fast that which is good.

Committal

Forasmuch as it has pleased Almighty God of his great mercy to take unto himself the soul of our dear brother/sister [name], we therefore commit his/her body to the ground; earth to ashes, dust to dust, in sure and certain hope of the resurrection to eternal life through Jesus Christ our Lord. Amen.

Closing Prayer

May the road rise up to meet you; may the wind be always at your back; may the sun shine warm upon your face, the rain fall soft upon your fields, until we meet again; may God hold you in the palm of his hand. Amen.

Blessing

Go forth into the world in peace. Be strong and of good courage. Hold fast that which is good. Love and serve the Lord with singleness of heart, rejoicing in the power of the Holy Spirit, and may the blessing of God Almighty, the Father, the Son, and the Holy Spirit be upon you this day and always. Amen.

✒ Chapter Nine

MEMORIALS

It is natural that many people, after the death of a loved one, will want to make some kind of physical expression of their love for the deceased person. This is, of course, the role that a funeral fulfills for most people. Even the simplest of funerals gives some ritual or rite, which enables those who are bereaved to show in actions what their words cannot express. Even the carrying of a coffin into a church or chapel with reverence does this. The clothes that are worn by mourners can be important for many people, signifying either the solemnity of mourning or the joy of thanksgiving for a life well lived. During the service itself there may be flowers on the coffin, the coffin may be sprinkled with water, people may bow toward the coffin, and candles may be lit to symbolize the prayers that have been said for the deceased. All these things are part of the process of remembering and giving thanks for the person's life and are part of the healing process which is necessary for those left behind.

Even the simplest of funerals gives some ritual or rite, which enables those who are bereaved to show in actions what their words cannot express.

In one sense, all these physical expressions of love and respect at the funeral memorialize the person who has died. Though the person is no longer alive, nevertheless people wish to show that the person's life and death were important to them. Many wish to continue expressing such feelings some time after the death. In their homes, photographs of the deceased may take on a greater prominence. Outside the home, the marking of the grave with a headstone is a common and ancient way of erecting a memorial. The rest of this chapter will look at the history and expressions of memorials and will suggest ways in which healing by memorialization can take place.

HISTORY OF MEMORIALS

Remembering the dead is an important part of mourning a loved one. The phenomenon is not new. Neither is it confined to any one part of the world. One has only to look at the huge number of stone circles and burial mounds that still exist in the U.K. today and which date from what are called by some "the Dark Ages" to realize how there seems to be a basic human need to bury the dead with dignity and then to create a memorial by which to remember them. In Mexico, the Day of the Dead is celebrated with families taking picnics to the graves of dead loved ones where they both talk about the deceased and clean their graves. In China there is an annual national day of mourning to visit graves, honor ancestors, and remember the dead. Japan has the festival of Tor-Nagashi each August where the dead are remembered at Lake Matsue, with floating lanterns bearing the family name on one side and a prayer on the other. In Brazil, on New Year's Eve, a similar ceremony takes place on Copacabana beach.

Having acknowledged these examples, we can see then that remembering the dead is not just a Western, Christian, or even modern phenomenon. In the Western Christian tradition, however, the remembering of the dead has traditionally focused on one particular day. In the late ninth century, Abbot Odilo of Cluny in France ordered that November 2 should be observed by members of his religious order as All Souls' Day. This local observance spread and soon became popular throughout Europe. On All Saints' Day (November 1), the church in the West remembers all those who had such remarkable and holy lives that it regards them as saints. The following day the church remembers all those who lived a life of faith, both those whose faith was known and those whose faith was known to God alone. Many churches in the U.K. hold special services on November 2 when names of the departed are read out as part of the liturgy. These names include those given to the minister by members of the congregation and the names of those congregants who have died in the last twelve months. At such services there is often the chance to light a candle in memory of a loved one, giving physical expression to the remembrance that is taking place in the heart.

At such services there is often the chance to light a candle in memory of a loved one, giving physical expression to the remembrance that is taking place in the heart.

MEMORIALS AFTER BURIAL

Burial in a Cemetery Plot

For many people purchasing a cemetery plot is the first step to creating a fitting memorial for a loved one. It is important to think carefully about the sort of cemetery plot one wants. Consider the location and check out the various restrictions the cemetery might place on you. Some have rules about the type of monument or memorial allowed; others restrict flowers being placed on the grave.

Consider the location and check out the various restrictions the cemetery might place on you. In a city, a cemetery plot can be expensive. In addition, you can expect to buy a grave liner. The casket will be lowered into the grave liner, which is placed in the ground before the burial. As the casket deteriorates, there is a risk that the ground will cave in. To prevent this, the grave liner (which is made out of reinforced concrete) stops the erosion. There are other costs. There will be a charge for opening the grave and then filling it in. And there will be some sort of groundskeeping charge to ensure appropriate care for the cemetery plot.

Having decided on the location, the next issue is the wording on the memorial. Naturally it is important to have the name and the years lived. Many Christians opt for a verse from Scripture. Others want to stress a particular relationship—the much loved father or husband. In each case memorial wording marks the life and honors it appropriately.

Some cemeteries prefer "lawn graves," with a flat headstone and no other marker on the grave. Such graves make maintenance of the grass simpler. Other cemeteries, however, permit great latitude in what marks a grave. In recent years, the erection of a mausoleum over a grave has been granted in some cemeteries. Mausoleums allow for a number of coffins to be entombed above ground and are not so dissimilar to those tombs, erected centuries ago, which can still been seen in old churchyards.

Cremated Remains

For cremated remains, one popular option is to purchase a crypt. This would apply if you want the ashes placed in a mausoleum or columbarium. When purchasing a crypt there are opening and closing fees, as well as charges for endowment care. This provides an opportunity to mark the place of the remains.

Some crematoriums inter cremated remains, not only in separate plots in lawns, but also in flower beds and under trees. Ashes may be placed either under existing plants or trees or perhaps under those planted specifically to commemorate the deceased. Plaques, either on the plant or nearby, can be erected. Both crematoriums and cemeteries dedicate benches in memory of those whose ashes are interred nearby. Requests for such memorials are not always granted, however, as these places would be overrun with places to sit down!

Other Memorials

For many generations, the only way to remember a deceased loved one was to erect and then

132 CHRISTIAN HOPE, CHRISTIAN PRACTICE

subsequently visit a grave. In our own age of fast and widespread communication, memorialization could hardly be easier.

There are now a number of Internet websites that are dedicated to creating and preserving electronic memorials to loved ones. One of the oldest and most popular is run by a computer science teacher at the University of Newcastle (http://catless.ncl.ac.uk /VMG). At this Virtual Memorial Garden, visitors can find "a place where people can celebrate their family, friends and pets and tell the rest of us about them and why they are special." At another site (www.cemetery.org) visitors can post whole pages of memorials, including pictures and words, as well as text, for a one-time fee. Should you wish, you can even "purchase" a star, which is then named after a loved one (www.international-star-registry.org). For instance, the star map designation Hercules RA 16h 56m 32sd 38 long. 15 lat. is named after a former police officer Larry T. Young.

A less exotic form of memorial is to make a charitable donation in memory of the loved one.

A less exotic form of memorial is to make a charitable donation in memory of the loved one. Funeral directors will usually collect such money if given around the time of the funeral and will pass it directly to the charity. Normally they will not charge for this service. A good way of advertising that you wish for money to be given to a charity is to include notice of this in obituaries in newspapers ahead of time. Remember that if the gift is made to a registered charity, it is tax deductible. This adds to the value of the donation. Some people, especially those who have been prominent in public life, may have a charity set up in their name after their death. This, though, will involve a lot of administration and is best done with the assistance of professionals in the field—accountants and solicitors.

REMEMBERING

As well as gravestones and the other kinds of memorials we have described, there are additional helpful and popular ways of remembering a loved one. Many people find it helpful to make a scrapbook of their loved one's life. This can be looked at in sad times to help those left behind cope with their loss. As well as including pictures and cuttings of the person's life, such a scrapbook can also include stories about the deceased and perhaps poems that have touched the heart of the person who is making the book (or even poems that they have themselves written about the deceased). Some people find it helpful to make a tape of favorite music, which reminds them of their loved one or helps them through death. It might also be possible to collect clips of the person's life on a video. This may be especially helpful if there is no grave to visit or little opportunity to make a physical expression of the loss that is felt. Those who are housebound, for instance, may find this particularly helpful.

Whatever form of memorial you choose, it is important that you feel the memorial is appropriate for you. Just as there is no such thing as the right way to grieve, neither is there any one right way to remember. Some find it helpful to talk to others about the deceased, while others prefer to keep silent. While some find listening to sad songs to be unhelpful, others find that this brings comfort and peace. Whatever remembering is done and whatever memorialization takes place as part of this, it should be real and helpful to those involved and should not be done in response to pressure from others or for the sake of doing what convention demands.

CONCLUSION

The purpose in thinking about death is to appreciate life all the more. Sensitivity to the fragility of life and, ultimately, to passing should help one cherish each and every moment. Christians believe life is a precious gift. Part of its preciousness lies in the relationships we forge. As we appreciate the finite nature of life, so we should appreciate all the more the smile of a child, the laughter of a friend, and the reflective story from an elderly relative. We need to learn to listen; we need to concentrate on the moment.

Death means dying, and often it means pain and bodily deterioration. Those of us lucky enough to live in the affluent West start to imagine that a normal earthly life is a pain-free existence. However, the reality of death and its surrounding processes remind us that this is just not the case. Once again as we reflect on death, we value all the more those moments when we are granted good health. Our underlying disposition should be one of gratitude.

The purpose in thinking about death is to appreciate life all the more.

Much of life involves pain. It hurts so much to see a loved one suffer. Many human lives are not pain free; sometimes people grapple with real and fundamental pain. One thing we have tried not to do is explain why life is like this. We have not attempted to answer the puzzle of theodicy (why a loving God allows pain and suffering). Instead of explanations, we have suggested trust. Instead of trying to puzzle it all out, we have suggested focusing on the creator God, who Christians believe died at the hands of the creation on a cross.

Our plea at the end of this book is this: Let us allow the reality of death to shape our underlying disposition to life. Let us be grateful for the gifts of good health, friendship, love, laughter, and beauty. And as the reality of our mortality creeps upon us, let us learn to trust and hope in the creator God who has given us these moments of being.

We have no choice but to walk this road together. We hope and trust that this book is a help on your journey.

And finally we urge you to "use" this book. We are not inviting you to agree with everything. Instead, treat it like a conversation partner. Our goal is to encourage thought and prayer. Feel free to take all particular ideas and arguments as discussion starters. You are entitled and invited to disagree with the book. As we think about death, we confront one of the ultimate mysteries of life. We are seeing through a glass darkly. We have no choice but to walk this road together. We hope and trust that this book is a help on your journey.

NOTES

FUNERALS AND DEATH

1. Douglas J. Davies, *Death, Ritual and Belief* (London: Cassell, 1997).

2. Davies, *Death*, 33–34.

3. Davies, *Death*, 82. Davies is at this point summarizing J. P. Parry, *Death in Banaras* (Cambridge: Cambridge University Press, 1994).

4. Davies, *Death*, 83.

5. Richard Dawkins, "Religion's Misguided Missiles," *Guardian*, 15 September 2001.

CHRISTIANITY AND DEATH

1. Keith Ward, *The Battle for the Soul* (London: Hodder & Stoughton, 1985), 152

2. Jürgen Moltmann, *The Way of Jesus Christ: Christology in Messianic Dimensions* (London: SCM Press, 1990), 254-56.

FINANCIAL MATTERS

1. The information in this chapter was partly compiled using the following books: Stephen Maple, *Wills and Estates* (2d ed.; Indianapolis: Alpha Books, 2003); Randell C. Doane and Rebecca G. Doane, *Death and Taxes* (Ohio: Swallow Press/

Ohio University Press, 1998); John Ventura (ed.), *The Will Kit* (2d ed.; Chicago: Dearborn Trade Publishing, 2002); and *Funerals: A Consumer Guide*, issued by the Federal Trade Commission.

2. Websites are useful ways of finding out the latest rules and regulations concerning financial matters. As in all things, however, no website ought to be taken as the final word on financial advice, and they should, therefore, be used in conjunction with professional advice from a human being sitting in front of you!

MUSIC, READINGS, AND PRAYERS

1. Henry Scott Holland, "The King of Terrors" in *Facts of the Faith* (London: Longmans, 1919).

2. Victor Hugo, "The Ship," in *Toilers of the Sea* (New York: Harper & Brothers, 1867).

3. Christina Georgina Rossetti, "Remember" in *The Oxford Book of English Verse: 1250–1900* (ed. Arthur Quiller-Couch; Oxford: Clarendon, 1919).

4. Percy Bysshe Shelley, "Music, When Soft Voices Die" in *The Oxford Book of English Verse: 1250–1900* (ed. Arthur Quiller-Couch; Oxford: Clarendon, 1919).

GLOSSARY

Throughout this book we present the material relating to funerals and end-of-life decisions as clearly as we can while still explaining as fully as is possible all the complex choices that need to be made. There may be some words or phrases, however, that either we have used or are used by others or contained in their procedures and documents, which are unfamiliar to you. To help you through this particular maze of jargon, we have compiled below a list of specialized words and a brief explanation of their meanings.

Ashuary

A place for the common burial of cremated remains after they have been kept for a period in a vault or columbarium.

Backfill

To fill in and cover a grave with earth immediately after burial of a coffin or casket.

Bier

A moveable frame on which a coffin or corpse stands before burial or cremation. Also the support for carrying a coffin or corpse to the grave.

Burial ground

A wide-ranging term for a place of burial. It may be the ground around a place of worship or a cemetery.

Casket

In the USA the word is used to denote a coffin that has sides, which are rectangular rather than tapered.

Catafalque
A structure on which a coffin or corpse lies during a funeral service or a lying-in-state.

Cemetery
A place used for burial, usually a large public area.

Cenotaph
A monument to honor a person who is buried elsewhere. The word comes from Greek, literally meaning "empty tomb."

Chapel of rest
Originally an undertaker's mortuary, the term now more generally means a place where a body is kept before a funeral and where it may be viewed. Used in such a way, chapels of rest exist in many hospitals.

Charnel house
A place, especially a vault, where dead bodies or bones are piled and stored.

Chest tomb
Sometimes called a box tomb, a stone or brick box built over a grave.

Churchyard
An enclosed ground, surrounding a church, used for burial.

Coffin
A box, usually made of wood but sometimes of metal, in which a corpse is buried or cremated.

Coffin-plate
A plaque on the lid or foot end of a coffin detailing the name, dates, and perhaps other information relating to the deceased.

Columbarium
A place of storage with shelves or niches for caskets of ashes, which may either be on display or sealed with plaques marking individual plots.

Common grave
A single place of burial of more than one corpse, usually without memorialization of individuals buried in the plot. These are to be

found where warfare or widespread disease has led to a large number of people dying in a short period.

Consecrated ground

A plot of land that has been dedicated and blessed by a bishop and which is set apart for the burial of the dead or their cremated remains.

Cremated remains

The calcified remains of a body that has been cremated. These are usually passed through a cremulator.

Cremator

A machine that cremates a coffin and corpse by means of flames and high temperature.

Crematory

The place in a crematorium where the cremators are to be found.

Cremulator

A machine that reduces the calcified remains of a body to a powder after cremation.

Deposition

When used in relation to a corpse this is the act of burial in the ground or placement in a mausoleum or catacomb. When used in relation to cremated remains this may mean either the scattering of ashes, the interment of ashes or the placement in a columbarium, mausoleum or catacomb.

Disbursements

The fees payable as part of a total funeral package, which are set by those other than the funeral director (minister's fee and crematorium fee, for instance).

Eulogy

The homily or sermon given at a funeral, which speaks in praise of the departed.

Exhumation

The removal from the ground of a corpse previously buried.

Footstone
A small, upright stone memorial set at the foot of a grave giving details of the deceased and perhaps other information, prose or poetry.

Funeral director
An alternative, and increasingly common, name for an undertaker.

Funeral parlor
The business premises of a funeral director.

Garden of remembrance
A piece of land, often adjoining a church or crematorium, which is set apart as a memorial to the departed. It may have individual or communal memorials giving the names of those being commemorated and may also be a piece of land in which ashes are interred.

Grave
A place in the ground in which a corpse or corpses have been or are to be placed.

Gravestone
A memorial placed on a grave. It may be either upright or placed flat on the grave.

Graveyard
A plot of land adjacent to or belonging to a church or chapel that is used for the burial of corpses or cremated remains.

Headstone
An upright stone memorial placed at the head of a grave with an inscription relating to the deceased.

Hearse
A car or carriage used to carry a coffin at a funeral.

Inhumation
The burial of a corpse, usually in a coffin, in the ground.

Interment
The burial of a corpse or cremated remains, especially with prayers or other ceremony.

Kerbset

The long pieces of stone that border a grave. They may surround turf and/or flowers, stone chippings or a body stone.

Landing stone

The large piece of stone or concrete that is placed on the top of a grave to act as a base for a monument.

Ledger

Also called a body stone, this is a piece of stone that totally covers a grave. It is also the term for the top of a chest tomb.

Lych gate

A wooden, gable-roofed gate at the entrance to a churchyard. Originally these were used as a temporary shelter for the bier during a funeral and part of the funeral liturgy took place here.

Mausoleum

A large and stately building designated as a place of burial or entombment of corpses or cremated remains, most often reserved for a particular family.

Memorial

A wide-ranging term for a sign or monument to a deceased person or group of people.

Memorial garden

A plot of land set aside as a place of remembrance for the departed, in which cremated remains may or may not be interred.

Monument

A general term used to denote a structure or building erected to commemorate a dead person or group of people, or a particular event.

Mortuary

A place where dead bodies are kept for a time, most often immediately prior to a funeral with attendant burial or cremation.

Ossuary

A vault or other storage place for the common burial or storage of bones of the dead, i.e. another name for a charnel house.

Pall

A large piece of heavy cloth, often made of velvet, which may be spread over a coffin at a funeral. Most often a pall is purple or black in color (the color of penitence and mourning) but sometimes it is white (signifying resurrection).

Pall-bearer

A person who helps to carry (or, more properly "shoulder") a coffin at a funeral.

Pascal candle

A large candle, kept in many churches, which is first lit at Easter each year and also lit at services of baptism. It may stand alongside a coffin during a funeral as a reminder of the Christian faith into which the deceased had been baptized.

Pedestal tomb

Similar to chest tomb but taller and narrower and not necessarily flat-topped.

Plaque

An engraved tablet affixed to a wall or set into the ground, giving the names, dates and perhaps other details of the departed who are commemorated or interred in a memorial garden or garden of remembrance.

Sarcophagus

A large stone coffin, often with additional sculpture or engravings.

Table tomb

A raised body stone, which is held up at its four corners by small pillars, which themselves stand on a landing stone.

Tablet

A small, flat slab of stone, metal or wood that has details of a deceased person or group of people, or event, inscribed upon it.

Tomb

Used in two senses, to denote either a place of burial or the monument erected over the place of burial.

Tombstone

Originally the stone cover of a coffin, the word is now more commonly used when talking of the large horizontal piece of stone covering a grave or a memorial over a tomb.

Undertaker

A professional person whose business is to arrange funerals and their associated requirements, also known as a funeral director.

Urn

Another, older, name for a casket that contains cremated remains. It is also the name for a piece of decoration found on some monuments, headstones or memorials.

Vault

An enclosed chamber, usually underground, set aside for the burial or entombment of corpses or cremated remains.

Vigil

From the Latin word meaning "to watch," a vigil is the time before a funeral, usually the night before, when prayers and other devotions are said for the departed.

Wake

A watch or vigil, most often held before a funeral, at which mourners share memories of the deceased.

Walled grave

Although most graves are simply dug from the earth, the coffin is interred and the grave backfilled, some graves are lined with brick, stone, or concrete. This may be so the grave is more easily opened up again for another, subsequent burial.

USEFUL ADDRESSES

On a number of occasions throughout this book, we mention that many of the inquiries or questions you may have concerning funerals and their arrangements will be easily dealt with by local funeral directors and clergy. If you are unclear about any of the issues dealt with in this book, or indeed about anything concerning funerals, please do not hesitate to contact them. However, if for some reason you require further information and advice, the following list of agencies may prove to be useful.

Alliance for Aging Research
2021 K Street, NW Suite 305
Washington, DC 20006-1003
202-293-2856

> To order your free guide, *Health Care Option Under Medicare: The Choice Is Yours*, write to Alliance for Aging Research.

American Association of Retired Persons (AARP)
601 E. Street, NW
Washington, DC 20049
202-434-2277
800-424-2277
Email Address: member@aarp.org
Internet Address: http://www.aarp.org

This organization has a focus on quality of life for the elderly. It can help with educational materials, assistance to the homebound, and advocacy.

Americans for Better Care of the Dying
4125 Albemarle St., NW
Washington, DC 20016
202-895-9487

This is a charity that aims to bring about policy reform to help improve the services for patients with serious illness.

Assisted Living Federation of America
10300 Eaton Place, Suite 400
Fairfax, VA 22030
703-691-8100

If you need a listing of member-assisted living organizations, then this organization can help you.

American Self-Help Clearinghouse
St. Clare's Health Serivces
25 Pocono Road
Denville, NJ 07834-2995
973-625-9565
TDD 973-625-9053

The American Self-Help Clearinghouse provides a national directory of more than 4,000 local self-help groups.

Center for Attitudinal Healing
33 Buchanan Drive
Sausalito, CA 94965
415-331-6161

Email Address: cah@well.com
Internet Address: http://www.healingcenter.org

> Among various services, this Center provides an AIDS hotline for kids, counseling, and support groups.

Center To Improve Care of the Dying RAND
1200 S. Hayes St.
Arlington, VA 22202-5050
703-413-1100
Email Address: CICO@rand.org

> As the name implies the focus is on educational activities that might improve the care of the dying.

Children of Aging Parents
1609 Woodbourne Road, Suite 302A
Levittown, PA 19057-1511
215-945-6900
800-227-7294

> This organization can provide information on caregiving issues and housing. It can also put you in touch with a support group.

Compassion in Dying
6312 SW Capital Hwy
Suite 415
Portland, OR 97201
Voicemail: 503-221-9556
Email Address: infor@compassionindying.org
Internet Address: http://www.CompassionInDying.org

> All the dilemmas surrounding the end-of-life options are handled by this organization, including pain management, hospice care and even aid-in-dying advice.

Compassionate Friends, National Headquarters
P.O. Box 3696
Oak Brook, IL 60522-3696
630-990-0010
Internet Address: http://www.compassionatefriends.org

The focus of this organization is the tragic death of a child.

Cremation Association of North America
401 North Michigan Avenue
Chicago, IL 60611
312-321-6806
Internet Address: www.cremationassociation.org

This is an assocation of organizations that offer a cremation service, including funeral homes, cemeteries, and crematories.

Department of Veteran Affairs
Office of Public Affairs
Washington, DC 20420
202-273-5700
Internet Address: http://www.va.gov

For veterans, this can be a very helpful resource.

Funeral & Memorial Societies of America
P.O. Box 10
Hinesburg, VT 05461
800-765-0107

This is a non-profit organization with local chapters around the country. It also provides a funeral price survey.

Funeral Consumers Alliance
PO Box 10
Hinesburg, VT 05461
800-458-5563
Internet Address: www.funerals.org

> This is a nonprofit organization that helps with consumer protection. The website is also the best source for Memorial societies; these are non-profit organizations that individuals can join to help them organize low-cost funerals.

Funeral Ethics Association
215 South Grand Avenue West,
Springfield, Illinois 62704
www.fea.org

> An organization that mediates in the event of a dispute.

Funeral Net
Internet Address: http://www.funeralnet.com

> This is a very helpful website. It covers almost all the issues surrounding funerals, cremations, and cemeteries.

International Order of the Golden Rule
13523 Lakefront Drive
St. Louis, MO 63045
800-637-8030
Internet Address: www.ogr.org

> Some 1,300 independent funeral homes belong to this organization.

National Selected Morticians
5 Revere Drive, Suite 340

Northbrook, IL 60062-8009
Internet Address: www.nsm.org

This is a national association of funeral firms that comply
with a Code of Good Funeral Practice.

Glendale Memorial Nature Preserve
Internet Address: http://www.glendaleatpreserve.org

Good resource on information for alternatives to traditional embalming and burial.

Heritage Funeral Home and Crematory
508 N. Government Way
Spokane, WA 99224
509-838-8900
Internet Address: http://www.heritagefunerals.com/questions.html

A resource for many of the commonly asked questions regarding cremation.

Living Will Registry
523 Westfield Ave.
P.O. Box 2789
Westfield, NJ 07091-2789
1-800-548-9455
1-908-654-1919 Fax
Email Address: admin@uslivingwillregistry.com
Internet Address: http://www.uslivingwillregistry.com

Information on organ donation, living wills, advance di-
rectives and health care proxies.

Memorial Ecosystems
Email Address: information@memorialecosystems.com
Internet Address: http://www.memorialecosystem.com

Information on ecologically safe ways for families to approach and make decision on burial and death.

Sinai Chapels
162-05 Horace Harding Expressway
Fresh Meadows, NY 11365
1-800-446-0406
Email Address: Sinai@jewishfunerals.com
Internet Address: jewishfuneral.com

Answers questions about Jewish burial and funeral ceremonies.

Temple Akiba
5249 S. Sepulveda Blvd.
Culver City, CA 90230
310-398-5783
310-398-1637 Fax

This organization is especially helpful to those needing advice on Jewish ceremonies.

Tri-Country Memorial Funeral Society
(Orange, Riverside, San Bernardino)
P.O. Box 114
Midway City, CA 92655
714-962-1917